3/06

Schmitt

100+ ESSENTIAL
FOR TEACHERS

CONTINUUM ONE HUNDREDS SERIES

100+ **ESSENTIAL LISTS**
FOR TEACHERS

Duncan Grey

continuum
LONDON • NEW YORK

CONTINUUM

The Tower Building	15 East 26th Street
11 York Road	New York
London SE1 7NX	NY 10010

www.continuumbooks.com

First published in 2005

British Library Cataloguing-in-Publication Data
A catalogue record for this book is available from the British Library.

ISBN: 0–8264–8718–1 (paperback)

Typeset by RefineCatch Limited, Bungay, Suffolk
Printed and bound in Great Britain by
MPG Books Ltd, Bodmin, Cornwall

CONTENTS

INTRODUCTION

I've always made lists. As a child I copied my grandma who organized her life with lists and as a teacher with an erratic memory I tried every method of list-making: on paper, sticky notes and electronic to-dos, to get through the day's tasks. Judging from the popularity of the first edition, I'm not alone!

Lists can be prompts to remind us, development zones for inspiration or scaffolding to arrange our thoughts. They are an efficient way of putting across a series of points stripped bare of ornament. They can inform succinctly in a small space and hint at broader fields beyond. They help us focus on priorities.

There were 100 lists in the first edition, three have been deleted and twenty added to this second edition. If you have a list you'd like to contribute to a future edition of *100+ Essential Lists for Teachers*, please send it to me at duncan@putlearningfirst.com and I'll consider including it in the third edition. Any list used will be gratefully acknowledged in future editions.

Duncan Grey
Cambridge 2005

Looking After Yourself

1

My personal list

- ○ Name ....
- ○ Address ....
- ○ Home phone number ....
- ○ School's phone number ....
- ○ Home email address ....
- ○ School's email address ....
- ○ Home fax number ....
- ○ School's fax number ....
- ○ Internet password hint ....
- ○ Network password hint ....
- ○ Head of department's phone number ....
- ○ Head of department's email address ....
- ○ Line manager's phone number ....
- ○ Line manager's email address ....
- ○ Key colleague's phone number ....
- ○ Key colleague's email address ....
- ○ Phone number for leaving work in absence ....
- ○ Caretaker's phone number ....
- ○ Burglar alarm number ....
- ○ Financial account numbers ....
- ○ Childminder's telephone number ....
- ○ Spouse's telephone number ....

Education is not the filling of a bucket, but the lighting of a fire. W. B. Yeats

LIST 2   Stress symptoms

Physical symptoms

- O Headaches and migraines
- O Sweating and palpitations
- O General aches and pains, and lethargy
- O Muscular tension
- O Colds and other respiratory infections
- O Asthmatic attacks
- O Raised cholesterol level
- O Digestive tract disorders and ulcers
- O Increased blood pressure
- O Thyroid disorders
- O Diabetes
- O Menstrual disorders and possible effects on pregnancy
- O Heart disease
- O Increased risk of cancer

Mental health

- O Irritability and depression with increased risk of suicide
- O Withdrawal
- O Tearfulness and anxiety
- O Poor concentration and forgetfulness
- O Disturbed sleep and insomnia
- O Low self-esteem
- O Post traumatic stress disorder – 'burn-out'

Behavioural symptoms

- O Heavy drinking and smoking
- O Misuse of drugs
- O Eating disorder
- O Poor timekeeping and increased sickness absence
- O Increased accident rate
- O Deterioration in personal relationships

Unless you try to do something beyond what you have already mastered, you will never grow.   Ronald E. Osbom

LIST 3   **Causes of stress in teachers**

- Excessive work load
- Excessive working hours
- Rising class sizes
- Pressures from Ofsted inspection
- Changes in courses and curriculum
- Changes to assessment and testing requirements
- Poor management
- Workplace bullying
- Crumbling schools
- Pupil misbehaviour
- Risk of violence from pupils, parents and intruders
- Lack of support with bureaucracy, form filling and routine tasks
- Lack of job security due to redundancy and fixed-term contracts
- Lack of control over the job
- Burden of providing cover
- Threat to early retirement arrangements
- Denigration of profession by politicians and media
- Lack of public esteem

(from *Tackling Stress in Teachers*, National Union of Teachers, 2000)

One test of the correctness of educational procedure is the happiness of the child.　　　　　　　　　　　　　　　　　　Maria Montessori

Stress busters 1 – quick ones

The classroom can be a very stressful place. These exercises are for when you've left the classroom.

- Get up and look out of the window. For one full minute look at something so closely that you could describe it in detail.
- Stand up and do some stretching exercises.
- Close your eyes and imagine your favourite fantasy.
- Close your eyes and deliberately relax one muscle at a time, starting with the top of your head and finishing at your toes.
- Close your eyes and re-live your greatest achievement.
- Close your eyes, imagine a relaxing beach scene, then breathe in the sea air in regular deep breaths.
- Take off your shoes and wriggle your toes, one at a time; then all of them.
- List ten things that you'd most like to do this week, this year or in your lifetime. Keep the list readily available so that you can remind yourself.
- Take a walk – the quieter and more attractive the place the better. Try some of the activities listed above at the same time.

It is the supreme art of the teacher to awaken joy in creative expression and knowledge. Albert Einstein

Stress busters 2 – longer term solutions

○ Try to surround yourself with pleasant and comforting things, such as flowers and green plants.

○ Keep at least one day of the weekend free from work. Avoid taking work home at least one night per week.

○ In the evening, allow time to switch off before going to bed. Read something lightweight for ten minutes or so.

○ Avoid working just for the sake of it. Ask yourself 'what would be the worst thing that could happen if I didn't stay late?'.

○ Assess new tasks by how much stress they may produce. Be prepared to say no to additional jobs.

○ Make goals realistic and achievable.

○ Have a 'to do' list and visibly cross things off when done.

○ Relax at lunchtime as often as possible. Regularly working through lunchtime gives no time for stress to subside.

○ Delegate where possible. A support assistant might take over at the front of the classroom; a parent might undertake some routine administration jobs; pupils may feel valued if given some regular small responsibilities.

○ Within a department or a management team consider which tasks are best rotated and which are best to supervise from a distance.

○ Say thank you often, genuinely and publicly to those who deserve it. Don't do this as a thoughtless routine.

○ Don't deal with stress by:
   – drinking too much coffee, alcohol or by smoking
   – losing your temper with people.
   If you have a confrontation ask yourself how you might have prevented it, don't automatically blame them. How might you have coped on a less stressful day?

At the desk where I sit, I have learned one great truth. The answer for all our national problems – the answer for all the problems of the world – comes to a single word. That word is 'education'.　　　　Lyndon B. Johnson

Stress busting for others

○ Actively help your colleagues.

○ If you are stressed or depressed, you may wish others appreciated you and your work. Try to do that for others.

○ Make a cake or buy some biscuits and share them with your colleagues at break or lunchtime.

○ Find out when your colleagues' birthdays are and bake them a cake or buy them chocolates.

○ Greet people with a smile.

○ Store up cheerful quotations or jokes, newspaper extracts or emails. Tell them or send them to someone who would appreciate it.

○ Mention colleagues' recent activities as examples of great teaching or professionalism.

○ Publicly pass on any positive mention of colleagues by pupils.

○ Listen to your colleagues. Let them speak.

The important thing is not to stop questioning.   Albert Einstein

Voice maintenance

○ Remember that a teacher is a professional voice user.

○ Look after your voice and learn to use it well.

○ Your voice is a vital element of successful teaching.

○ Your voice can convey your mood.

○ Pupils can sense nervousness and stress and can play up to that.

○ Women teachers with high-pitched voices should try to cultivate deeper calmer voices.

○ Teachers are at risk because:
  - teachers have to use their voices every working day
  - there is little or no rest-time allowed
  - voices are used in noisy environments with poor acoustics against background noise.

○ Drink at least six glasses of water per working day. Dehydration causes damage to voices.

○ Avoid dairy products (including chocolate), strong alcohol, strong coffee, fizzy drinks. Don't smoke.

○ Avoid rushing lunch or eating late in the evening (acid indigestion is bad for the vocal chords).

○ Stand with a straight back, knees relaxed, eyes looking forwards rather than upwards.

○ Avoid coughing and shouting as far as possible.

○ Avoid speaking for long periods in noisy environments.

○ Avoid dry and dusty environments (use dry markers on whiteboards rather than chalk on blackboards, ban cigarettes from the staffroom).

○ Don't shout. Use alternative methods of gaining the attention of classes (a ticking clock drawn on the board, hand in the air and visibly counting, clicking your fingers at two second intervals . . .).

Thou hast most traitorously corrupted the youth of the realm in erecting a grammar school. William Shakespeare (King Henry VI, pt 2, act 4, sc. 7)

Hints for a healthier you

Don't

○ slump in front of a computer screen
○ spring up too quickly after bending down to talk to a pupil
○ carry loads which are too heavy (and that includes piles of books)
○ smoke or drink too much coffee
○ drink too much alcohol if you're stressed
○ use holidays as a time to catch up on work
○ neglect family and friends
○ imagine conscientiousness is always a good thing
○ rush everywhere.

Do

○ get out more – an evening stroll, cycle or walk to work
○ park away from school and walk in, if you have to drive
○ take lunch or break outside when it's fine
○ take short breaks from marking to rest your eyes and inflate your lungs
○ have green plants, natural light and humidifiers
○ eat breakfast
○ have a healthy lunch and make it a real break
○ sip water throughout the day
○ walk about and stand evenly on both feet
○ take a break before an after-school meeting
○ take an evening class in something that is not connected with your classroom
○ have a regular well-being check-up
○ arrange holidays well in advance
○ get a good night's sleep.

The most important contribution schools can make to the education of our youth is to provide them with a sense of coherence in their studies; that is, a sense of purpose, meaning, and inter-connectedness in what they learn.
Neil Postman

Getting Prepared

 Preparing for the start of term

○ Order materials for next term in the light of curriculum needs.
  – display materials
  – background resources for reading, display work, etc.
  – stationery
  – audio-visual – OHPs, spare bulbs, extension lead, etc.
  – computers – check with the technician before the end of term for anything that might require repair or new software
  – worksheets
  – furniture – is repair or recovering required? Is it adequate for the age and the numbers of pupils?
○ Clear out the mess from last term: do this at the end of the old term if possible.
○ On the last day write a list of important tasks to do before next term. Fold it and put it away with your school keys until the end of the holiday.
○ Buy new clothes, get a hair cut, replace worn things.
○ Compile a diary and calendar.
○ Timetable: make copies for your diary, the notice board and for home.
○ Class lists and registers. Create systems for recording observations on pupils.
○ Start learning pupils' names, use photographs if available.
○ Classroom: consider decoration, storage, the security of equipment, green plants and reference information.
○ Display: rotas of responsibilities, charts of processes, lists of spellings, number sequences, topic-related items . . .

Most students have no idea of the true joys of learning, and of how much they can actually achieve on their own.   Adam Robinson

Advice on joining a new school

○ Don't talk about your last school. Rephrase all suggestions as 'I wonder if we could . . .?' rather than 'In my last school we . . .'.

○ Listen rather than talk. Judge the atmosphere before you impose your views.

○ Look around the staffroom before sitting in a seat. That's true literally as well as metaphorically.

○ Ask polite/naïve questions rather than searching/intrusive ones.

○ Don't be cynical. Even established staffroom cynics don't like new cynics.

○ Listen to everyone. Caretakers, cleaners, office staff, technicians and supervisors are all sources of information, knowledge and wisdom. Filter and balance their views, but listen to them all before making a judgement.

○ Notwithstanding the above, be clear about who the prime movers are. Who mobilizes opinion, influences, solves problems, answers questions, etc.

○ Confirm and consult your line manager(s) and assure yourself of what you must do if things go wrong.

○ Listen to the pupils too. Their expressed views are significant in the way the school works. Even when they are wrong it's important to know what they think.

○ Pay your dues promptly – to the staffroom fund, the coffee kitty, etc.

○ Be seen around, but don't get locked into any particular group. Groups may have an agenda which can work against fairness and openness.

○ Get keys so you don't get locked in, or out.

○ Be punctilious about duties, meetings, timetables, prompt arrival at lessons, response to requests, etc.

○ Learn people's names and roles as soon as possible. Borrow a school photo if necessary.

○ Join in on an equal basis. Concerts, socials, breaktime buns, whatever – play your part. Later you can pick and choose.

○ Dress conservatively. Staff costume is often earned by subject, status or character. Wait until you have read the situation sensitively.

- ○ Check on the way you should address colleagues and governors. First names? Mr/Mrs? Take particular care when pupils are around.
- ○ Look carefully at informal practices as well as what is written in the staff handbook:
  - – What is tolerated uniform (shirts hanging out of trousers; rings)?
  - – What is enforced (litter; out-of-bounds areas)?
  - – What is accepted (offering a replacement pen to a pupil; a note excusing the wearing of trainers)?
  - – What punishments are routinely meted out for what offence (after school detentions; lunchtime detentions; extra work; litter picking)?

Do not believe what your teacher tells you merely out of respect for the teacher.   Guutama Buddha

Making a worksheet

Purpose   What's the point? Start with purpose and work towards appearance.

Curriculum level   Consider the reading age, the age of maturity, the Key Stage, the programmes of study and the topic.

Content   Search for relevant quotations, maps, graphics, references and illustrations. Check the copyright.

Language   Use active, not passive; simple sentences; key words; headings and subheadings; avoid rhetorical questions; ask clear and understandable questions; match with the reading level; use sidebars or boxes for specialist vocabulary and bullet points for clarity.

Medium   Choose the most appropriate from: a black and white photocopiable A4 sheet; a colour returnable handout; OHT; a booklet; a web page; a multi-media presentation; a disposable; something to be written on and retained. Consider card, lamination or a booklet.

Design   Should enhance the content not obscure it; limit the range of fonts; use a consistent graphic style; use a simple invisible grid; use bullets and boxes for key points; make navigation clear, use arrows and numbers consistently.

Product   What do you want in the end? Is the message clear? Provide a range of tasks to suit a variety of learning styles; offer choice where possible; include short-answer questions and open-ended tasks; include homework research, individual and group work tasks.

Trial   Treat the worksheet as a draft to be improved; observe class queries, confusion and comments; revise a paper worksheet at the same time, then apply the comments to the computer file as soon as possible.

Storage   Store paper copies methodically for easy retrieval; consider filing cabinets, trays, plastic pockets in split ring folders. Mark a master copy with a red dot; ensure that the master copy is never given out. Store computer files in a methodical file structure with coherent file names.

Universal education is the most corroding and disintegrating poison that liberalism has ever invented for its own destruction.   Adolf Hitler

LIST 12 Top teaching tips

There is no one right way to teach. But you do have the right to teach.

- Call students by their names.
- Give students specific, incremental steps to learning something.
- Know your subject.
- Listen to your students as individuals.
- Find ways to make students responsible for their own learning.
- Remember that being active not passive helps learning.
- Make lessons relevant by associating them with pupils' own experience.
- The priority is that pupils work hard, not you.
- Always have a backup idea.
- Be prepared – and expect the unexpected.
- Always have your students' best interest at heart.
- Have confidence and control at all times.
- Have patience. Then more patience. And then some . . .

Of course, Behaviourism 'works.' So does torture. Give me a nononsense, down-to-earth behaviourist, a few drugs, and simple electrical appliances, and in six months I will have him reciting the Athanasian Creed in public.

W. H. Auden

Hints for surviving 'the inspection'

The inspector will be looking to see if the teacher:

○ Shows good subject knowledge and understanding in the way that he/she presents and discusses his/her subject.
○ Shows technical competence in teaching the basic skills.
○ Plans effectively, setting clear objectives that pupils understand.
○ Uses time, support staff and other resources, especially information and communication technology, effectively.
○ Assesses pupils' work thoroughly and use assessments to help and encourage pupils to overcome difficulties.
○ Uses homework effectively to reinforce and/or extend what is learned in school.

Prepare yourself for this by:

○ Planning your lessons to explicitly show these criteria.
○ Showing evidence of your planning.
○ Collecting examples of your outcomes.
○ Including statistics.

Curiosity is one of the most permanent and certain characteristics of a vigorous mind.   Samuel Johnson

Setting work for absence

○ Remember that you are writing for a non-specialist who may not even be interested in your subject.

○ Make the task and instructions clear and unambiguous. Write the main part so that it can be read directly to the class: 'You should do . . ., then turn to . . .'. Give clear page and chapter numbers for text books.

○ Make clear where books, stimulus material and equipment can be found and where it can be returned to.

○ State whether the class should have their exercise books and their text books with them or that they will be provided.

○ Make the key parts simple and brief enough to write on the board – or produce a worksheet for each pupil.

○ Give follow-up work for those who finish.

○ Give guidelines so that the cover teacher will know what is expected and what is not acceptable.

○ Make the product clear in terms of content and length and say whether it must be handed in at the end of the lesson or completed for homework.

○ Provide a set list and space for comments on the lesson, pupils and their behaviour.

Later . . .

○ Find out who covered your lesson. Thank them.

The authority of those who teach is often an obstacle to those who want to learn.   Cicero

Christmas fun list

Make as many words as you can   From (e.g. name of the school, local town with a minimum of ten letters, Christmas Day, etc.). Rules: words must be in the available English dictionary, no fewer than four letters, s plurals don't count as extra.

Pictionary   Divide the class into two teams (boys v. girls is usually best); on slips of paper each team provides names of books, songs, musical performers, popular phrases, etc.; the slips are placed in random order at the front of the class; team members come up in turn to select a slip from the other team's pile; they have to draw the item on the board; team members have to guess the name or title; points for speed, for example three points for a name guessed in 30 seconds, two in under one minute, one in under two minutes. Appoint a timekeeper from each side, or time it yourself. Make a prominent score board. Award prizes at the end for the best drawings.

Wordsearch   Give out a photocopied grid of say 10 × 10 squares; pupils write in the squares words connected with Christmas, a minimum of, say, 30 words, each in a straight line, written in any direction then fill in the remaining squares with random letters. Pupils write clearly their name and the precise number of Christmas words hidden in the grid. Hand completed grids to teacher. First finished swaps with second finished etc., drawing from the collection at the front. Completed grids with a line drawn through the entire word to be returned to the owner for checking.

Twelve Days   Remind pupils of the song *The Twelve Days of Christmas*:

> On the Twelfth Day of Christmas, my true love gave to me:
> Twelve Drummers Drumming, Eleven Pipers Piping, Ten Lords
> A-Leaping, Nine Ladies Dancing, Eight Maids A-Milking,
> Seven Swans A-Swimming, Six Geese A-Laying, Five Golden
> Rings, Four Colley Birds, Three French Hens, Two Turtle Doves,
> And a Partridge in a Pear Tree.

- – ICT – use copy and paste to produce each verse in its entirety.
- – English – write letters from the young man's 'true love' in which she thanks him for the gifts, but becomes increasingly stressed at the constant delivery of crazy presents to her door. The letters should show increasing fury.

- Maths – if, on the second day, the young man were to send a further partridge as well as two turtle doves, on the third day yet another partridge, two more turtle doves, as well as the three hens, etc., calculate how many of each item would be sent. Express this in graphic and numeric form.
- Art – draw the scene of devastation (above); design Christmas cards using some of the verses; design stained glass (coloured tissue) windows featuring the items in the song.

Using behaviourism to control learning is like using an umbrella to control the weather. Steve Nordby

Lesson planning

An eight-step model

○ Intro: a short activity to help focus on the main lesson. A handout, a question or brief task written on the board.
○ Purpose: the objective of the lesson, why are we doing this?
○ Input: vocabulary, skills and concepts, what we need to do this.
○ Show: demonstration of the final product, what we will have by the end of this.
○ Follow me: guide the pupils through the stages necessary to perform the skill, this is the way we do this.
○ Check understanding: questions to confirm learning, do you understand this?
○ Independent practice: do it yourself.
○ Closure – wrap up the lesson: this is what you've learned today.

A six-step format

○ Content: concept, skill, subject matter.
○ Prior knowledge and skills: what they need to know before they can learn this.
○ Instructions: description of what pupils will actually do.
○ Materials and equipment: list the kit and how it will be used.
○ Evaluation: describe how you will evaluate the success of the lesson.
○ Self assessment: How did you do? What might you have done better? What will you do next?

Common lesson planning mistakes

○ *Objective* is unclear. What's the point? What will they do and why?
○ *Assessment* is unrelated to the lesson activity.
○ *Prior knowledge* and skills are vague, wrong, missing or inappropriate.
○ *Materials and resources* are unnecessary or unrelated to the task.
○ *Instructions* are long winded. Be brief, organized and efficient.
○ *Student activities* do not effectively relate to learning objectives.

A poor surgeon hurts one person at a time. A poor teacher hurts 30.
Ernest Boyer

In the Classroom | 3

LIST 17 — Things you need in your bag

This will vary according to age range, subject specialism, whether you are on supply or are permanent.

- ○ J-cloth to clean the board
- ○ Coloured felt tips for writing on paper
- ○ Coloured dry whiteboard markers
- ○ Chalk
- ○ Coloured pencils
- ○ Spare HB pencils
- ○ Eraser
- ○ Pencil sharpener
- ○ Blu-tak
- ○ Blank and lined paper
- ○ Exercise books
- ○ Pritt-style glue
- ○ Scissors
- ○ Tissues (noses and leaks)
- ○ Red pen
- ○ Stapler
- ○ Drawing pins
- ○ Keys if necessary
- ○ Lesson scheme
- ○ Lesson plan
- ○ Emergency lesson plan
- ○ Collection of short stories at appropriate level.

What wisdom can you find that is greater than kindness?

Jean-Jacques Rousseau

Learning pupils' names

Knowing pupils by name creates successful relationships and effective discipline.

- Prepare class lists beforehand. Make a mental note of interesting names. It's never too early to start learning them.
- Make a set of pupil photographs for each class from your school management system or your own photograph.
- Use a seating plan and stick to it.
- Add photographs to the seating plan.
- Don't add personal notes or descriptions of physical features to the seating plan if there is any chance of pupils or parents seeing it.
- Learn about the naming conventions and common pronunciations of different linguistic and cultural groups.
- Use names. Refer to the seating plan. Avoid pointing.
- Consider using name cards on desks for the first few lessons.
- Give back written work yourself to help you associate names and faces.
- Test yourself until you are confident you can link a name to a face.
- Consider making a memory game called 'Test the Teacher' and compete for memory success with the pupils.
- Use traditional memory devices such as:
  - repetition
  - flash cards
  - using several senses when memorizing: speaking, gesturing
  - visualize the classroom and methodically identify the pupils as they sit. Associate the names with pictures and in your mind place those pictures incongruously along a route you know well. Follow the route methodically and recall the pictures. So by your garden gate there is a brown bear with an angel's halo recalling Angela Brown, on the zebra crossing stands Alice in Wonderland kicking a dent in your car wing to recall Alice Denton, etc.
- Remember that in large schools not even all pupils will know everyone in the class.

You cannot teach a man anything. You can only help him discover it within himself.   Galileo

Giving instructions for a classroom activity

Get maximum attention   Stop all questions, stand very still, look sternly at everyone, stand at the focal point in the room, direct the pupils to look and listen, use a firm tone of voice.

Make learning objectives explicit   Make objectives relevant and important, make them understandable, explain how they will be evaluated and what will be done with the product.

Provide a visual focus   Move around while remaining in view, use obvious hand movements, use the whiteboard, write main points clearly and boldly, use different colours for different categories and headings, draw pictures if they illustrate points effectively.

Explain resources   Provide a task sheet or worksheet; have pupils write down items from your board list and add their own too; suggest where they might find answers; point out opportunities for further research; be clear about the parameters of what is allowed, and what is forbidden; be specific about written style; be specific about whether handwritten or using a computer.

Give examples   Involve people by giving relevant examples, bringing in their own experience, working through the process so that they can see what they have to do.

Give the opportunity for questions   Circulate the room inviting individual further questions as they begin the task.

Allow some time for settling   Brief reassuring conversations with partners can be helpful.

Enforce silent or quiet work   Even five unbroken minutes will set things in progress. 'If there's any talk at all we'll start the five minutes again . . .' establishes your need for concentrated work.

We're going to have the best-educated American people in the world.
Dan Quayle

Speaking and listening topics

Topics to describe Tying a shoelace; a spiral staircase; a new set of clothes; a member of your family; where you stayed on your holiday; my perfect boy/girl friend; a memorable journey; my happiest moment; the best thing I ever made/repaired; my greatest sporting moment.

Contentious topics

- Should hunting be banned?
- Should school uniform be abandoned?
- Should smoking be banned for under 18s?
- Do we still need marriage?
- Computers will take over the world. What should we do?
- Should sex and violence be banned from TV?
- Hold a balloon debate in which each participant has to justify him or herself in order to avoid being thrown out of the balloon.
- Who would be the last two people in the world? Take the part of a famous person and defend your right to be one of the last people to stay in the safe nuclear bomb shelter. There has to be one man and one woman and they have to have enough in common to make it possible for the human race to continue!
- Medical experiments on animals should be stopped.
- Boys and girls are not the same, so they are not equal. What rules should apply to one gender, but not to the other?
- Adults know best; children should know their place.

Brainstorming topics Alternative means of transport; alternative ways of learning; ways to enforce maximum attendance at school; ways to save ourselves from the end of the world; things to put in a survival pack; ways to make money legally.

Speaking to different audiences

Topic	Alternative audiences
Welcome to our school	Parents, new teachers
Help us raise money	Local traders
Young people are not so bad	Parents, teachers, the police, local politicians
Cars damage the environment	Local traders, local politicians
Give us better bus services	Bus company, local politicians

Failure is not the worst thing in the world. The very worst is not to try.   Anonymous

Speaking and listening activities

○ Speak to the group for four minutes on a topic about which you are interested.

○ Tell a story to the class – something that happened to you.

○ Have a short question and answer session.

○ Describe awkward things without using your hands.

○ Describe a picture or a drawing to a partner who is sitting back to back with you and see if they can replicate it.

○ Using a matched set of Lego bricks, one team describe to the other what they have made while the other tries to replicate it without seeing it. Discuss the difficulties experienced.

○ *Pictionary* describe an object without naming it or key words associated with it (this is available as a commercial pack).

○ A debate with proposers, seconders and a participating audience, on a contentious topic.

○ Brainstorming:
  1 Work in groups of four to six.
  2 Collect as many answers and comments as possible.
  3 Delete the obviously ridiculous.
  4 Pool the remainder to provide a class list for general discussion.
  5 Place them in rank order.

○ Talk for one minute to the class then talk for one minute on the same topic, as if there were a different audience. It can help to face the opposite direction for the second talk.

○ Discuss a topic in your own group of four to five, then one member moves on to another group to summarize your discussions and findings to them.

Keep trying, it's only from the valley that the mountains seem high.

Zeig Zeigler

Emergency lessons with no equipment

Assume that pencils, scrap paper and preferably a board and pen or chalk are available.

Compile 5 × 5 crosswords as shown below:

Clues should be definitions.

1		2		3
	■		■	
4				
	■		■	
5				

Down:

1

2

3

Across:

1

4

5

A survey For example, TV viewing habits, preferred entertainment, school subjects liked/disliked, etc.

○ Ask the questions and record the results.
○ Draw graphs and charts.
○ Write a report of the results.
○ Suggest implications, consequences, actions, etc.

School improvements Discuss different kinds of school buildings, organizations, curricula, activities, etc.

○ List ideas in note form.
○ Draw and design a new school, which would take advantage of the new ideas discussed.
○ Design a poster and/or leaflet to advertise the new school.

Write an A–Z Words connected with a certain subject. For example, musical instruments and terminology, scientific discoveries and inventions.

○ In words or pictures define or illustrate a word so that it is easily understood.

Brain. n. An apparatus with which we think that we think.

Ambrose Bierce

LIST 23   Questions for a pupil-to-teacher interview

○ How are you getting on in [subject]? Do not say with . . . [teacher].
○ What's your favourite subject? Why?
○ What's your least favourite subject? Why?
○ What would you like to do when you leave school?
○ What subjects/grades do you think you need for that?
○ What's your favourite way of learning? (Reading, listening, doing, sharing with others, working alone/in groups, etc.)
○ What would you say are your best skills/qualities?
○ If you were in my shoes, what would you change?
○ How could we, together, make things better for you at school?
○ If you were head teacher what would you do?
○ What makes you happiest/unhappiest about a school day?
○ What is the biggest problem in the way of you being really successful at school? Can we get rid of it or get round it? How?

The only person who is educated is the one who has learned how to learn and has changed.   Carl Rogers

Final products – more than just copying out . . .

Here are some subject alternatives for the dull 'Write a report on . . .' or the dangerous 'Find out everything you can about . . .'.

---

advertisement
art gallery
arts festival
autobiography
banner
book review
brochure
cartoon
collage
courtroom trial
debate
demonstration
diagram
diary
display case
exhibition
experiment
fact file
flag
flip chart
flow chart
game
heraldic shield

journal
lesson
letters
machine
magazine
model
mural
museum
musical instrument
news bulletin
picture book
poster
PowerPoint presentation
puppet show
scrapbook
song
time capsule
time line
TV or radio commercial
verdict
videotape
web page

The real voyage of discovery consists not in seeking new landscapes but in seeing with new eyes. Marcel Proust

LIST 25   Books you'll both approve of: popular fiction for young people

Year 7 and 8 pupils

Male

- ○ *White Out; Held to Ransom; Biker; Extreme Survival; Drop; Daring Escapes* – Anthony Masters
- ○ *Mossflower* – Brian Jacques
- ○ *Uncanny (Even More Surprising Stories); Unseen* – Paul Jennings
- ○ *The Hobbit* – J. R. R. Tolkein
- ○ *More Horowitz Horror* – Anthony Horowitz
- ○ *Harry Potter and the Philosopher's Stone; Harry Potter and the Chamber of Secrets; Harry Potter and the Prisoner of Azkaban; Harry Potter and the Goblet of Fire; Harry Potter and the Order of Phoenix; Harry Potter and the Half-Blood Prince* – J. K. Rowling
- ○ *Star Wars: Heir to the Empire* – Timothy Zahn
- ○ *Boy Tales of Childhood; The Twits* – Roald Dahl
- ○ *Wings* – Terry Pratchett
- ○ *Loudmouth Louis; Bad Dreams* – Anne Fine
- ○ *Iron Fist* – Aaron Allston
- ○ *Solitaire Mystery* – Josteain Gaarder

Female

- ○ *How To Survive Summer Camp; Double Act; Lizzie Zipmouth; Girls in Love; Lottie; Twin Trouble; Clubbslyme; The Illustrated Mum; Sleepovers; Girls Under Pressure; Vicky Angel; Girls Out Late* – Jacqueline Wilson
- ○ *Princess Diaries; Princess Diaries Take Two* – Meg Cabot
- ○ *California Diaries* – Dawn-Ann M. Martin
- ○ *There's a Boy in the Girls' Bathroom* – Louis Sachar
- ○ *Spoonful of Jam* – Michelle Margorian
- ○ *Are You There God It's Me Margaret; Here's To You Rachel Robinson* – Judy Blume
- ○ *Criss Cross* – Susan Gates

Children have never been good at listening to the elders, but they have never failed to imitate them.   James Baldwin

Easing the workload

Marking is important. It is a vital part of assessment and an acknowledgement that pupils' work is worthwhile. It can also be time-consuming, stressful and sometimes dispiriting. How, apart from a derisory 'tick flick' can it be prevented from eating into your life?

○ Adopt peer marking. Pupils mark each others' work, using a checklist provided by the teacher, and add a signed positively critical comment.
○ Set tasks, especially homework tasks, which require minimal marking. These include:
  – drawings
  – diagrams
  – preparation for oral presentations
  – display work
  – reading
  – learning spellings
  – background research.
○ If a task is a presentation in front of the class, use oral feedback from yourself and the class.
○ Target marking: tell the class in advance that you are particularly going to look at one aspect of their writing, for example spelling, presentation, punctuation, description.
○ Set reading homework which requires an oral reading response or can be checked by a brief question and answer session.
○ To save time, ask pupils to leave the exercise books open at the page.
○ Mark projects at the time that they are being written – one-to-one teaching while the class works. Treat a series of tasks as one assignment.
○ Encourage drafting and redrafting. A good exercise in itself and one which produces a single final good quality product. It is better to set a few pieces done well rather than piles of poorly executed work.

What sculpture is to a block of marble, education is to the soul.
                                                              Joseph Addison

Spelling hints

○ A silent E on the end of a word makes the vowel in front say its name (mat-mate).
○ E after C makes it sound S (face).
○ E after G makes it sound J (rage).
○ The sound NS at the end of a word is usually spelled NCE (fence).
○ Drop the E if you add ING (hope-hoping).
○ F, L and S are doubled after a single vowel in a one syllable word (till but not until).
○ ALL, WELL, FULL, TILL always drop one L when added to another word (welcome, useful).
○ P, T, N and G are doubled after a short vowel and before adding an ending beginning with a vowel (shop-shopping).
○ K is spelled CK after a short vowel at the end of a one syllable word (clock).
○ CH is spelled TCH after a short vowel at the end of a one syllable word (watch).
○ If a word ends in a vowel + Y keep the Y before adding an ending (donkeys).
○ If a word ends in a consonant + Y change the Y to I before adding the ending (parties).

Twenty most common spelling mistakes in secondary schools

accommodate	necessary
address	niece
believe	payable
business	possible
definitely	receipt
embarrass	responsible
friend	rhythm
government	secretary
jewellery	separate
library	surprise

(according to Susan Rooney, published in the *TES* 10.12.04.)

An eye for an eye makes the world blind. Ghandi

Advice and help for supply teachers

- ○ Consider why you are doing supply work:
  - – Unemployment?
  - – Freedom and choice?
  - – Temporary bridge to other things?
  - – Because you hate marking and bureaucracy?
- ○ Bear this in mind when negotiating with schools.
- ○ Consider concentrating on a small number of local schools.
- ○ Consider going freelance rather than relying on an agency.
- ○ Make yourself known:
  - – Talk to staff at lunchtime and break.
  - – Report positively back on what you've taught and how the lesson went.
  - – Be discreet about what you see going on in different areas.
  - – Find out who makes decisions about cover.
  - – Be proactive about contacting the school.
  - – Thank the people who help you throughout the day.
  - – Remember names of pupils and staff.
  - – Don't forget you are a lowly person in the hierarchy.
- ○ Get to know the schools:
  - – Show interest in the school and its individuality.
  - – Build up a picture of the school compared with others.
  - – Share this with teachers only if they ask.
  - – Remember few teachers like their school criticized.
  - – Ask for a guided tour.
- ○ Approach each lesson on its own terms:
  - – Use the time between lessons to gather equipment and read instructions.
  - – Be prompt or even early to each lesson.
  - – Start each lesson as firmly and confidently as possible.
  - – Announce your name and write it on the board.
  - – Assert firm rules immediately.
  - – Don't make excuses for not knowing the subject matter.
  - – Take your list of emergency lessons everywhere.
  - – Add to your list of activities as you proceed.
  - – Build up a stock of useful portable resources.

A teacher affects eternity; he can never tell where his influence stops.
Henry B. Adams

LIST 29 Supply teachers' emergency kit

- List of lessons you are expected to cover
- Work set for each lesson
- Information on any problems likely to occur
- Set or class lists
- Lesson times
- School rules
- Handbook of basic procedures
- Fire and emergency procedures
- Map of school showing classroom numbers
- People to see:
  - for advice
  - to complain
  - to get your money
  - to get spare supplies
  - to refer to for lesson plans
  - to refer pupils to.
- Payment claim forms
- Packed lunch, tea and coffee, small change for staffroom coffee contribution
- Newspaper or personal reading material (for use at break or lunchtime)
- User name and password for any computer network
- ID – your own and what the agency and the school may give you
- A card showing your contact details, to ensure the school remembers you (if you want to go back).

To be fully prepared:

- dictionary
- atlas
- maths kit (protractor, compass, ruler, calculator)
- short story book appropriate to age
- list of emergency lessons.

Reading is to the mind, as exercise is to the body.   Richard Steel

Fifteen useless things pupils excel at

1 Count how many gobs of chewing gum there are on the bottom of the desk. Feel each one with a finger and shriek 'Eeeugh!' when they touch each one.

2 Rock back on their chair and see how far they can lean back until either the chair collapses under the strain or they lose balance and fall.

3 Amuse their friends by shrieking in mock pain until they fall off their chair.

4 Dismantle their only pen and make it leak ink all over the desk and their hands.

5 Persist in demanding that they be let out of the classroom to clean up.

6 Scream with pain and cross their legs shouting, 'I'm going to wet meself' until the teachers are forced to allow them to go to the toilet.

7 If a teacher ignores them, fling their pen down and slam their book closed screaming, 'If you're not goin' to help me I'm not doin' no work!'

8 If offered help by their teacher, fling their pen down and slam their book closed screaming, 'If you're goin' to get on at me I'm not doin' no work!'

9 Whenever they don't know what they are supposed to do, shout, 'These lessons is borin'.

10 Whenever they realize what they are supposed to do but don't want to do it shout, 'These lessons is borin'.

11 Take their neighbour's pencil case and systematically destroy it.

12 Ensure they bring no folder, books or pencil case. Make sure that they bring no pen except for the one destroyed earlier (see ploy 4).

13 Shout loudly complaining, 'I can't do no work cos I ain't got no pen'.

14 Always chew gum. If forced to put it in the bin they bite it into two or more pieces, putting one part in the bin, placing another part under the table (see ploy 1).

15 Always keep their coat on as long as possible. Emit deep sighs and groans if told to remove it. Complain it's cold.

The mind is a pattern-seeking device. Children who have been taught pattern will continue to hunt for solutions.   **Anonymous**

- A sudden gust of wind blew it out of my hand and I never saw it again.
- The lights in our house went out, and I had to burn it to get enough light to see the fuse box.
- Another pupil fell in a lake, and I jumped in to rescue him. My homework drowned.
- I used it to fill a hole in my shoe. You wouldn't want it now.
- My father had a nervous breakdown and he cut it up to make paper dolls.
- My pet gerbils had babies, and they used it to make a nest.
- I didn't do it, because I didn't want the other kids in the class to look bad.
- I made a paper plane out of it and it got hijacked.
- I lost it fighting this kid who said you weren't the best teacher in the school.
- I was mugged on the way to school and the mugger took everything I had.
- I put it in a safe, but lost the combination.
- I loaned it to a friend, but he suddenly moved away.
- Our furnace stopped working and we had to burn it to stop ourselves from freezing.
- I left it in my shirt and my mother put it in the washing machine.
- I didn't do it because I didn't want to add to your already heavy workload.
- My little sister ate it.

The most frequent and most likely to be true is:

- My computer crashed and I lost everything.

You may not be responsible for your heritage, but you are responsible for your future.   Anonymous

LIST 32 Behaviour and attention

Maintain interest by:

○ Planning a coherent lesson with a recognizable purpose.
○ Breaking a lesson into a variety of activities to maintain interest and momentum.
○ Establishing a simple and accepted way of gaining attention.
○ Making your message purposeful. Make use of their silent attention to give clear instructions. Never deliver a weak, vague or rambling message – it devalues the importance of their attention.
○ Giving clear instructions before an activity and avoiding interrupting positive activity with extra instructions.
○ Offer a choice of learning tasks where possible.
○ Link your work to their interests.

Minimize disruption at the beginning of a lesson by:

○ Providing a task immediately so they have something to do.
○ Enforcing a routine around seating plans, stowing bags and coats, readying equipment, calling the register.
○ Being there and watchful as they arrive.

Minimize disruption at the end of a lesson by:

○ Completing the lesson in time before the bell.
○ Giving out instructions and homework well in time.
○ Enforcing a routine around clearing up equipment, putting on coats and leaving in an orderly fashion.

Good ways to gain attention:

○ Stand facing the class, clap hands three times and stare out anyone who does not respond immediately.
○ Draw a clock on the board and explain that if there is no silence, minutes of the time wasted will be marked on the clock, leading to withdrawal of privileges.
○ Raise your hand and wait until all pupils have raised their hands and are silent.
○ Cultivate a teacher's stare (narrow unblinking gaze, scarily incisive).
○ Expect silence: you are more likely to get it.

Bad ways of gaining attention:

- ○ Physical assault on nearest pupils.
- ○ Aggressive threats.
- ○ Screaming in a high-pitched voice.
- ○ Showing fear.
- ○ Calling for help over trivial transgressions.
- ○ Threatening punishment which is not carried out (especially 'If you do that again I'll . . .').

Nothing has happened in education until it has happened to the student.
Joseph Carroll

Behaviour management

Everyone – teachers, non-teaching staff and pupils – has the right to:

- Learn
- Be safe
- Be treated with respect

- Everyone is responsible for their own behaviour.
- We all have a choice in how we behave.
- Criticise the behaviour, not the person.
- Teachers can, and should, earn respect.
- Teachers are role models for behaviour.
- There is no punishment so awful that it will force students to conform to teachers' wishes if they don't want to.
- Forming a relationship with pupils is essential.
- Behaviour management involves developing a range of responses to behaviour.
- Be proactive in teaching – head off inappropriate behaviour before it happens.
- Adopt a wide range of low-level strategies before a crisis occurs.
- Don't refer to previous events when dealing with current behaviour.
- Teachers should always remain in control of their emotions.
- Identify weaknesses and try to solve these before they contribute to behavioural problems.
- Know your students' names and use them.
- Care. If you don't care – leave.

Rules

- Schools need rules.
- Rules must be taught and upheld by teachers.
- Rules should be explained in a positive way.
- Rules should create a balance between rights and responsibilities.
- School rules are created to enshrine these rights.
- Rules must be an integral part of school routine.
- Breaking the rules will have consequences; the consequences need explanation.

Establish a small number of firm rules of accepted behaviour in class which are understood and accepted

Exclusion

○ Selective schools may exclude permanently; inclusive schools must consider the effect of exclusion.
○ Most children do want to attend school – though some may not wish to take part in all activities.
○ If a pupil consistently refuses to allow learning to take place or abuses the rights of others or their physical and mental safety, then they have *chosen* to relinquish their right to a place in the school.

I believe in standardising automobiles, not people.   Albert Einstein

Homework

Make homework positive

○ Avoid giving homework as a punishment.
○ Mark and return it promptly.
○ Provide feedback on the task.
○ Supervise peer marking of a straightforward homework task.
○ Make it relevant – to them and/or to the current teaching topic.
○ Integrate homework into the lesson by referring to and using it during the lesson.
○ Explain homework very clearly so there is no scope for confusion or excuse.
○ Avoid explaining homework at the end of the lesson among the disruption of clearing up.
○ Arrange in advance a time to *your* convenience when you can supervise any pupils whose homework has not been done.
○ Refer to the school homework policy.

A home opportunity

Use homework as an opportunity to bring in family, home and experiences outside school.

○ A questionnaire with views or reminiscences of neighbours on local history.
○ A survey of shopping outlets, traffic flow, television viewing habits.
○ A review of what their family thinks on a given topic as preparation for a class debate.
○ Surveys of local facilities.
○ Bring in examples of items related to a new class topic.
○ Interview the family for an autobiography, bring in photographs.
○ Research local sources for a project.
○ Include cooperative homework as an option, so neighbours or friends can work together.

Homework which involves parents and family can help at parents evenings. It makes parents feel part of what goes on in school. They can see it as their contribution to their child's education.

Give adequate time before homework is due. You will not endear yourself to a family with a busy life by insisting detailed research be in the next day.

Remember that not all families are well equipped to provide homework help. While some will have books, Internet access and be willing to drive a child to an area of interest, others may be unable to offer any help at all. Some may even actively discourage the child by their attitude or routines.

Homework diaries and planners

○ These are essential organizers.
○ They encourage independent learning and organizational skills.
○ They establish good study habits.
○ Insist that they are checked by parent and teachers alike.
○ Insist that all homework is written in, accurately, at the time it is given.

The beautiful thing about learning is nobody can take it away from you.
B.B. King

Avoiding plagiarism in pupils' work

○ Explain that while ideas are free, plagiarism is taking someone else's work and passing it off as your own.

○ Teach a whole lesson on plagiarism, pointing out the educational, moral and legal implications. Discuss the notions of fair use and intellectual property.

○ Demonstrate how ICT methods, including search engines, can reveal plagiarism. Enter a string of words in quotation marks to find a precise match or key words to find a more general match.

○ Tell students that you use anti-plagiarism websites such as www.plagiarism.com; www.plagiarism.org; www.wordcheck.com.

○ Teach the art of good writing. Point out that this is more valuable than any short-term benefit gained by copying someone else.

○ Use the phrase 'copying from one source is plagiarism but taking from several sources is research' to teach about synthesizing ideas from a variety of sources.

○ Insist on pupils acknowledging their sources.

○ Show your own skill at identifying copied work, for example, sudden changes in vocabulary levels and sentence complexity.

○ Avoid general instructions such as: 'Find out everything you can about . . .' Prefer specific instructions such as: 'Research life in Victorian times in order to write a day in the life of a young person your age in the last decade of the nineteenth century.'

○ Avoid clichéd essay titles, already written by many others.

○ Give interesting writing assignments which will be more likely to capture pupils' imaginations.

○ Give detailed instructions about using a specific framework.

○ Start drafting in lesson time. Show an interest in pupils' notes and early drafts and ask for drafts to be included with the final version.

○ Consider having pupils write an evaluation paragraph reflecting on the process of their writing. What they are proud of, what they had trouble with, what they learned from this assignment.

Education comes from within; you get there by struggle, effort and thought.
Galileo

LIST 36   The classroom environment

The school and classroom environment has a great impact on pupil behaviour and the effectiveness of learning. Teachers can't always expect to have a classroom for themselves but they can influence its arrangement.

○ Furniture may be fixed and therefore inflexible and uncomfortable for pupils of different shapes and sizes.
○ External distractions and noise at certain times of the day can disrupt learning.
○ Light and ventilation in rooms may not be adjustable and can cause discomfort.
○ Sight lines may be poor.
○ Classrooms may be cluttered and untidy, even dirty and dangerous.

From time to time take a moment to stand at the back of the class and view it from the pupils' point of view. Try this on the first day back after a holiday so you can see it relatively fresh.

○ Is the classroom cluttered and untidy or neat and well organized?
○ Are notices, rules and posters attractive and stimulating or dog-eared and fading?
○ Are chairs and stools comfortable for all those who use them?
○ Can heating be adjusted for comfort? Is the room ventilated?
○ Can lighting be adjusted for comfort? Are curtains or blinds adequate for the job all the year round and at all times of day?
○ Can heating and lighting be adjusted by pupils under supervision or must it be done by the teacher or caretaker?
○ Is the floor clear and clean or are there obstructions or wear?
○ Is equipment stored safely and retrieved easily?
○ Are desks and chairs in a position for pupils to sit comfortably and to:
  – write or make
  – talk in a group
  – get up, collect or perform, and return
  – see and hear the teacher
  – see the board
  – see a projection screen
  – see and hear a television screen.
○ Consider a seating arrangement which can be adjusted for different

needs and have pupils practise safely and efficiently moving them to a different arrangement (and back at the end of an activity).

Visit other teacher's classrooms and also consider what influences your impressions and mood at a doctor or dentist's surgery, a supermarket, an office or a home.

Consider the message sent to pupils by the environment you create – and what they will think of you as the host in that room.

The vastest things are those we may not learn. . . . How pitiful is our enforced return, to those small things we are the masters of.

Mervyn Peake

Good and bad questions

'The only stupid question is the one you don't ask'

But there are ways of encouraging questions in the classroom and ways of avoiding awkward answers.

Closed questions

○ May elicit recall: 'What is an escarpment?' 'What is the number of this element in the periodic table?' 'Who was the President in 1945?'

Effective quick-fire questions can increase alertness and test understanding, though they don't actually develop learning in themselves.

○ They may also be a bungled attempt to increase teacher–pupil interactivity: 'What do you think he was called?' 'Does anyone have any ideas?'

These include 'guess what teacher is thinking' questions and involve pupils hazarding random guesses in the hope of hitting a target which pleases teacher – or not.

Open questions

○ Can stimulate discussion and imagination, especially if they're building on shared knowledge and experience.

Stopping a narrative at a crucial moment and asking: 'What happens next?' can cause pupils to combine their knowledge of events and characters so far and imagine possible developments.

○ Can stimulate the imagination and could be the basis for a creative project.

Asking for possible uses for a brick or what use a castaway might make of a ball of string, a plastic carton, a car tyre and a wooden crate (for example).

○ Avoid too many broad or vague questions and vary the people you are addressing.

'Does anyone know anything about the Civil War?' Balance this
with either: *'Who can tell me about the causes of the Civil
War?'* and *'James, tell me what you know about the causes of
the Civil War.'*

○ Try to target pupils with questions they are likely to be able to
answer. This is differentiation and need not be condescending.

Organizational questions

These should:

○ narrow down the number of possible responses
○ be well focused and targeted
○ aim to limit simultaneous calling out
○ be rephrased as instructions rather than questions, where possible.

Don't ask: 'Does anyone need a ruler?' 'Does everyone
understand?'
Do ask: 'Who does *not* have a ruler?' 'Is there anyone who does *not*
understand?'
Don't ask: 'Is there anyone away today?'
Do ask: 'Put your hand up if you think there's someone from this
class not here today.'

Disciplinary questions

Don't ask: 'Where do you think you're going?'
Do ask: 'Where *should* you be?'
Don't use sarcasm: 'Do you want to poison us all?' 'How do you
expect to write without a pen?' 'Were you brought up in a field?'
Do ask: 'Turn off the gas tap. That's dangerous.' 'Bring in a pen for
next lesson.' 'Please close the door.'

We all learn by experience, but some of us have to go to summer school.
Peter de Vries

Discipline 4

Praise

If you are reading this list near the end of a grim, exhausting term, in the hope of finding a way out of a spiral of bad classroom relationships, these points may sound very shallow. Frankly it's probably too late!

Just as you have your views of this or that class, they have made up their own minds about you already too. Try afresh at the beginning of next term; try even harder at the beginning of next year.

○ Try to praise at least twice as much as you criticize. Praise can be: public – in front of the class; private – quietly to the individual; or official – by merit marks, notes to form tutor, messages to parents, mention in assembly, star charts, etc.
○ Read out good work.
○ Display good work (classroom walls, corridors, display cases, school foyer).
○ Publish good work (school magazine, intranet, website).
○ Display the names of good workers (classroom board, a prominent place in the school, in a letter to parents).
○ Use a merit award scheme and highlight the award winners regularly.
○ Praise participation even if not the content.
○ Plan something good or fun for the last few minutes of the lesson to reward class good behaviour.
○ Let the class know when they've been good.
○ Build bridges outside the classroom: on duty and between lessons talk in a friendly way, share a joke, ask opinions.
○ Prefer good natured humour to anger (if you can).

Why don't they pass a constitutional amendment prohibiting anybody from learning anything? If it works as well as prohibition did, in five years Americans would be the smartest race of people on Earth.   Will Rogers

Criticism

General criticism   Avoid criticizing or blaming the whole class for the misbehaviour of the few. Avoid saying things like 'You are the worst class I've ever taught', etc. In the unlikely event that this is true, it still doesn't achieve anything and may say more about your own state of mind.

Personal criticism   By all means criticize a pupil's behaviour – but not the pupil him/herself. For example, it is not helpful to use the word 'stupid', because the pupil will probably feel it is directed at him personally. 'Unacceptable behaviour' is always to be preferred to 'stupid boy (or girl)'.

- Use sarcasm very carefully. It may be witty to you but it can be hurtful to others.
- Don't belittle pupils. A moment's thoughtlessness on your part and they can remember it for ever.
- Never refer to race, belief or personal appearance critically.
- Keep a record of a pupil's bad behaviour. Describe it factually and unemotionally.
- If, on reflection, your record of pupils' behaviour reads to you as a list of trivialities, it may be that the pupil is strategic in his or her behaviour. Or it may be that you are prone to overreact. Think carefully about which of these is true before taking it further. Consult other teachers of the child.
- Make sure that you have an exit strategy, whether it's:
    - giving a punishment (extra work, a deadline, moving the pupil away from the source of discontent, public or private reprimand, withdrawal of privileges, detention)
    - helping (giving a pen, paper or equipment, taking the pupil outside the classroom for an individual talk, suggesting you talk to someone else on the pupil's behalf)
    - sending to a sin bin area
    - referring to the form tutor, year tutor or writing home.
- Make sure that you know the school procedures in cases of pupil indiscipline.

Grammar schools are public schools without the sodomy.   Tony Parsons

Rules

Be consistent   Pupils actually like to know where they stand and a consistent policy on your part helps them as well as you. While we should not have totally different rules for each person, we must recognize that different pupils respond to different strategies. It's this 'consistency with flexibility' which is the sensitive balancing act we tread from moment to moment.

Be fair but firm   Easier said than done, but most pupils respect that. Even if the child you are dealing with is utterly unreasonable, the rest of the class will expect you to remain rational, reasonable and fair, especially to them. That will be strongly in your favour in the future. Calm professionalism, however much it may hurt to maintain it, is more effective than incandescent rage. Keep the moral high ground, but don't be trampled on.

Physical violence   Never use physical violence. If it happens, report it and explain it immediately to a senior colleague. Use restraining techniques only in the very rare circumstance in which injury is certain to take place. This should be accompanied by you saying: 'I am holding you to restrain you and save you from injury. Stop and I will let go.'

- Remember that you can't change the world alone, though united with colleagues you might have an influence.
- Teachers need to look after themselves and each other. Support your colleagues, improve morale by listening, helping and sharing.
- Organize the classroom the way you want it. Set up a learning environment: seating, decoration, lighting, resources readily available and of good quality, wall displays, clear rules, etc.

Ever wonder if illiterate people get the full effect of alphabet soup?
John Mendosa

Routines

Establish routines for:

○ entering and leaving the room
○ getting the students' attention
○ establishing quiet working
○ asking for help
○ using and returning resources
○ homework
○ silent reading
○ using potentially dangerous equipment
○ doing a test
○ forgetting homework
○ losing a book
○ having no pen or pencil
○ uncooperative behaviour
○ not completing work
○ distracting others
○ forgetting a password.

Make your expectations and aims clear:

○ have a clearly defined core task, plus options and alternatives
○ give relevant examples
○ what students are expected to learn from the activity
○ what students should have produced by the end of the activity
○ where students are in the curriculum or examination course
○ how/whether the work will be marked, assessed or displayed
○ whether this is draft and preparatory work or course work
○ when work is due in
○ how long students have to complete it.

If a man is a fool, you don't train him out of being a fool by sending him to university. You merely turn him into a trained fool, ten times more dangerous. Desmond Bagley

Crime and suitable punishment

○ Don't threaten a punishment which you are not prepared to follow through.
○ If you can, enforce your will without public confrontation.
○ Bear in mind practicalities enforced by:
  –school buses
  –extracurricular commitments
  –school rules
  –school custom and practice
  –parental expectations
  –appropriateness of sanction to misdeed
  –the inadvisability of being on your own with a child.

A graduated scale of sanctions

○ Disapproving stare – the teacher's stare is a powerful though undervalued weapon (be careful about using it carelessly on small relatives).
○ Pause and wait for attention and conformity.
○ Make a specific demand as you walk past. Don't engage in eye contact. Show you fully expect the child to conform.
○ A sharp word using the pupil's name.
○ Repetition of the above in a firm but reasonable tone.
○ Specific demand: 'James, put that away.'
○ Repetition of the above: 'James, I have told you to put that away. Please do it **now**.'
○ Threat of punishment: 'Molly, I have asked you twice. If you don't put it away now I'll have to take it from you.'
○ Withdrawal of privileges.
○ Moving position of the child in the classroom.
○ Private talk after the lesson.
○ A brief removal from the room: 'Patrick, come outside the classroom with me. I want to talk to you about your behaviour.'
○ Detention: lunchtime, break or after school. Preferably supervised by yourself (inconvenient, but it can give you the opportunity to re-establish relationships).
○ Removal of the child to another place.
○ Removal of the child to another place by calling in a senior colleague.

- A phone call or letter home.
- An internal report, in which each lesson receives a grade or comment and the accumulation is monitored by senior colleagues or pastoral staff.
- Meeting with the parents.
- Internal exclusion.
- Exclusion.

Dublin university contains the cream of Ireland: Rich and thick.

Samuel Beckett

Rewards

Determine what is an acceptable reward and what might be embarrassing.

Thanks   Appreciated immediately following a good deed. A quiet word, a brief mention at the end of the lesson, a line in a school report.

Sweets   Popular but not always appropriate for a serious reward. Keep for class quizzes and as a light-hearted reward.

Party with pop and cake   Popular with younger classes who have done well collectively. Teacher must be prepared to join in the fun.

Watch a video   A typical end-of-term treat, but be careful. Choosing the right video is important. You must be sure it has the correct age certificate. Beware older pupils bringing in their choice.

Certificates   Suitably academic and easy to produce. Decide where and by whom it's appropriate to be presented.

Letter or phone call home   Too often letters or phone calls home are announcements of bad behaviour. For an outstanding contribution and recognition, a letter or call describing positive achievement, improvement or success is invaluable both for the pupil and for teacher–school relations.

School magazine or website   Reference to achievements in these forms of public media are sources of great pride. A photograph at sports day with a caption referring to the pupil's achievement, a reference to a willing helper, a performance on stage, all stay with pupils for a long time.

Reference to other teachers   An informal note or mention to another teacher can be surprisingly successful in boosting the pupil's confidence. 'Mr Grey was telling me you've done some great D&T work – well done', this is double praise.

Quite frankly, teachers are the only profession that teach our children.
Dan Quayle

Restraint and exclusion

Full details are given in a DfES circular of 10/98 (supplementary guidance 10/99), Human Rights Act.

○ Physical restraint should only be used as a last resort, however teachers may use reasonable force to prevent pupils from: committing a criminal offence; injuring themselves and others; causing damage to property (including their own); and engaging in behaviour which has a negative impact on maintaining good order and discipline in the school or on other pupils.
○ Do not feel obliged to intervene if your own personal safety is at risk.
○ Make every reasonable effort to summon assistance.
○ Use physical restraint only in exceptional circumstances.
○ Be warned that situations involving physical restraint can easily be misinterpreted.
○ All incidents should be reported as soon as is practical, to both the school and your union.
○ Each school should have a policy which outlines practical implications. Training should be available.
○ Permanent exclusion is likely to be appropriate for:
  – serious, actual or threatened violence against another pupil or member of staff
  – sexual abuse
  – presenting a significant risk to the health and safety of other pupils by selling illegal drugs
  – persistent and malicious disruptive behaviour, including open defiance or refusal to conform with agreed school policies on, for example, discipline or dress code.
○ The National Union of Teachers believes that:
  – malicious disruptive behaviour may include abusive and offensive language.
  – pupils who require physical restraint in anything other than exceptional circumstances should be excluded.

An encyclopaedia is a system for collecting dust in alphabetical order.
Mike Barfield

Misbehaviour strategies

Three stages of averting misbehaviour

○ Divert (ignore attention seeking, ask a question, move to a new activity, remove distractions).

○ Correct (eye contact, move closer to the pupil, naming the miscreant, praising someone else).

○ Warn (a specific warning which will lead to punishment if ignored).

Other strategies

○ Don't lose your temper. An angry child needs a calm teacher to regain control.

○ Be consistent. Pupils need to know the rules and the boundaries.

○ Maintain that consistency even when it's tempting to relax.

○ Criticize behaviour not the person.

○ Criticize specifics, not generalities.

○ Use genuine and specific praise whenever possible.

○ Build relationships outside of class too – clubs, sports, trips, lunch queues and break duty.

○ Consider making written behaviour agreements with pupils to address specific behaviour problems such as sitting down, listening, communicating with others.

○ Persistent low-level poor behaviour is a source of classroom stress. It is mainly predictable so try to prevent it in advance.

○ Emphasize the importance of team work – and the team includes you.

○ Enforce your right to establish seating arrangements from the beginning. Use it to separate miscreants.

○ Vary seating arrangements according to task.

○ Ensure all pupils are facing you and attentive when receiving instructions.

○ Encourage positive behaviour.

○ Try to be positive at least twice as much as you are critical.

○ Try to nip inappropriate behaviour in the bud.

If all else fails

○ Don't take all misbehaviour personally.

○ Don't get involved in public wrangling in front of the class.

- Agree a positive plan for the future.
- Keep to any agreements.
- Explain that you really want to help them to improve.
- Maintain respect.
- Stay professional.
- Record disciplinary events as evidence for all parties.

(From: www.teachernet.gov.uk/professionaldevelopment/
nqt/behaviourmanagement/behaviourtips/.)

Outside the Classroom

LIST 46 Planning suitable school trips

- ○ Trips should be beneficial to the pupil.
- ○ Trips may be directly relevant to the curriculum or may provide enhancement to the school experience.
- ○ A trip's aim should be made clear to participants (pupils and teachers) as well as to parents, governors and to teachers left behind covering your classes.
- ○ If the trip is compulsory and a coursework requirement, it will be seen in a different light to one which is recreational. Issues of cover, absence and cost contributions may therefore differ.
- ○ Let the trip be a chance to let the world into your classroom.
- ○ Be very vigilant on a trip; you are in *loco parentis*.

Be sure to ask yourself:

- ○ Why are we doing this?
- ○ What outcomes do I expect?
- ○ When do we leave and return?
- ○ Where are we going to?
- ○ What are we going to do there?
- ○ How are we going to follow this up?
- ○ How does this fit into the curriculum?
- ○ How can we make the most of it?
- ○ Is it an appropriate venue, date, task and journey?

What's another word for thesaurus?   Steven Wright

Preparing for the trip

Consult   Consult with the head or senior colleagues.

Dates   Check dates with the school diary.

Phones   Compile a phone tree with contact names.

Insurance
- Check travel and health insurance and confirm it is appropriate to your visit.
- Treat safety and insurance seriously.
- Check thoroughly with county/school/union guidelines, especially where there is any form of adventurous activity.
- Make an informed risk assessment.

Medical   Keep a list of medical requirements; receive signed permission from parents or guardians to administer medicines. Pack first aid kit tissues, sick bags, drinking water and any permitted medicines, labelled for each particular child.

Passports   Collect and keep safe all passports.

Book   Prepare and book the trip well in advance.

Deadlines   Give clear deadlines for payments or cancellation.

Money   Accounting; collect and record payments officially, giving receipts; check regulations for charging for school activities; offer hardship subsidy if appropriate.

Information   Arrange clear information sheets for all participants; arrange a meeting, at which questions may be asked and issues raised; include expectations; a detailed programme; emergency contact arrangements.

Permission   Have signed permission slips for activities.

Special needs   Make arrangements for pupils with special needs.

Set work   Leave work for any classes you may miss.

Prepare   Prepare and place the visit into context before the day.

You don't appreciate a lot of stuff in school until you get older. Little things like being spanked every day by a middle-aged woman: stuff you pay good money for in later life.   Emo Philips

○ Take a mobile phone. Give its number to a named link person at school.

○ Materials: provide spare writing materials, worksheets, etc.

Expectations

○ Make your expectations clear to pupils. Include behaviour; clothing; what they may and may not do; what will happen if they do not behave; bed times; check-in times; never to go off alone/ minimum group numbers. Police this rigorously. Include this in your written handout to parents. Check with the coach driver and hosts, if any, to determine their expectations too.

○ Know the children that you are taking with you.

○ Carry a definitive list of children and check it often. Always check the children getting on and off the coach and after every activity. Don't rely on asking 'Is there anyone missing?' but do arrange small buddy groups where children have some duty to look after each other; define a meeting-up place for every event.

○ Trust the staff or adults you are taking with you. Ensure that they are insured too. Confirm that child protection and criminal conviction procedures have been followed.

○ Check that everyone can get home safely if you arrive back late at school.

○ Make sure you know of any regulations applying to transporting children in your car, on the school minibus, or on other forms of transport.

I won't say ours was a tough school, but we had our own coroner. We used to write essays like: What I'm going to be if I grow up.   Lenny Bruce

Examination invigilation duties

- Read the exam officer's regulations thoroughly well before the exam and keep a copy with you for reference.
- Check:
  - Who is supporting you?
  - What do you do if a candidate wants to leave early or arrives late?
  - What if they need to leave the room briefly?
- Make sure that you know the timing and duration of the exam.
- Arrive promptly in the correct room with enough time to spare to cover contingencies.
- Check the clock is accurate, visible and working.
- Show start and finish times clearly.
- Ensure that there are enough exam papers, answer booklets, spare paper and any other permissible equipment for the number of candidates. Are there other rooms? Are other candidates being supervised elsewhere?
- Are there two consecutive papers and, if so, is the second paper available?
- Check the attendance of all candidates.
- Notify absences.
- Produce a seating plan.
- Ensure students have left superfluous clothes and equipment elsewhere.
- Mobile phones must be switched off.
- Maintain silence.
- Give out and collect papers and answer sheets.
- Stay alert.
- Check rubric on exam papers regarding timing and equipment. Check on reading time. Are calculators required?
- Prowl the gangways between desks checking for cheating of any kind.

'Come to the edge,' he said. They said, 'We are afraid.' 'Come to the edge,'
he said. They came. He pushed them. And they flew.   Apollinaire

Ways of staying alert

While you should not compromise your vigilance by any untoward activity, a total lack of activity can actually stun you. Some mental activity or limited writing coupled with a measured walk and a stern mask of vigilance can keep you alert.

If you're a people person

○ Try to identify as many of the candidates as possible and recall something about each one.

○ Predict the future prospects for any of the candidates you can identify – rocket scientist, novelist, criminal . . . Then devise a quote for each character when the press interview their old schoolteacher.

○ Imagine that you are a terrorist. Plan the demise of a shortlist of deserving pupils.

If you're a words person

○ Write a list of things to do a) for school b) at home. If necessary, redraft the list in order of importance.

○ Take in a photocopy of the quick crossword from your staffroom newspaper and try to complete it in the time available.

○ Write a poem using only the words available in the 'notes for invigilators' sheet.

○ Write a comedy sketch based on the questions and tasks in the examination paper. The characters might have an informal or amorous conversation, but speak only using formal examination language.

○ Plan an adventure story beginning 'If I had not gone into teaching I would have . . .'.

○ Construct your own crossword: a 5×5 grid or greater.

○ The following are anagrams of National Curriculum. Place each one in a sensational newspaper story:

OUTRUN RUNIC CAMILLA
CLOUT CRANIUM URINAL
CRUCIAL URINAL MOUNT
INTO ANAL CURRICULUM

If you're a numbers person

Calculate some of the following, individually or in combination:

○ How many days you've been teaching.
○ How many days you have left:
  a) in this year
  b) in total.
○ Your earnings:
  a) today
  b) every day of the summer holidays
  c) since you started teaching
  d) until you retire.
○ Your outstanding mortgage:
  a) in total
  b) per year
  c) per day.
○ The value of your home:
  a) as it has risen or fallen since you bought it
  b) as it could rise or fall until your mortgage is paid off
  c) as it could rise or fall until you sell it
  d) as profit or loss to you per year, week, day, invigilation session.

It is only the ignorant who despise education.   Publilius Syrus

The five Ps of presentation

Preparation Have all seating and furniture in place, check lighting and sound, make printed and display materials ready, check all projection equipment is working, greet the audience, know your stuff.

Purpose Be clear about the aims of your presentation, what the audience expects and make it practical and focused.

Presence Be confident, assured, knowledgeable, relaxed.

Passion Be forceful and committed about your subject.

Personality All the above plus a measure of humour and modesty!

A good presentation for teachers:

○ Never begins with an apology.
○ Gives practical information for classroom use.
○ Concentrates on the personal experiences of the audience and gives the help they need.
○ Finishes promptly with a summary of what has been said.

A good presenter

○ Is up-to-date with his/her material.
○ Is prepared and organized.
○ Has a sense of humour.
○ Makes the audience think and relate to the topic.
○ Presents, rather than reads from notes.
○ Presents and interprets rather than reading from OHPs or slides.
○ Interacts with the whole audience.
○ Finishes on time.

The mediocre teacher tells. The good teacher explains. The superior teacher demonstrates. The great teacher inspires. William Ward

Ways of involving visitors

- ○ Give the visitor clear directions and instructions.
- ○ Have pupils prepare and ask questions. Use the key question words who, what, why, where, when and how as prompts.
- ○ Ask your visitor to bring in some objects as evidence for what he or she does. The visitor will feel more confident in their discussion and the pupils will have a focus.
- ○ Prepare your own questions, in addition to inviting the children to ask theirs, but don't take over – give them a chance.
- ○ Discuss beforehand what the visitor is happy to do or talk about, to avoid embarrassment.
- ○ Decide beforehand how much you want to let the visitor do. Some may need coaxing, others would like to take over. It's your classroom.
- ○ Take a back seat if all is going well.
- ○ Make your timing clear – prompt arrival and departure are important.
- ○ Reinforce requirements of behaviour with the children beforehand. Emphasize appropriate language. Explain courtesy.
- ○ Have a child, or two, collect the visitor from the lobby or office. Practise a form of words with which they will introduce themselves.
- ○ Provide refreshments wherever possible. Younger children might like to serve a drink or a cake; older pupils may be happy to have the visitor disappear to the staffroom.

Teaching is the profession that creates all others.　　Anonymous

Harassment and bullying

Harassment by someone else is not your fault! You may feel guilty, but it is important not to automatically accept the blame.

Harassment has been defined as 'improper, offensive and humiliating behaviour, practices or conduct, which may threaten a person's job security, create an intimidating, unwelcoming and stressful work environment, or cause personal offence or injury' (*Workplace Bullying: Report of NASUWT Survey of Members 1995*, National Association of Schoolmasters and Union of Women Teachers, Birmingham).

○ Make sure you are a paid-up member of your trade union or professional association.
○ Talk to someone to ensure you keep the problem in perspective. Don't bottle up your feelings.
○ Consider using your union representative as an intermediary.
○ Record the details of each incident accurately and unemotionally. Individual small incidents may be part of a significant series with an overall impact.
○ Tell the bully you want it to stop: either write to them (and keep a dated copy), or have a reliable professional friend, such a union representative, do so on your behalf.
○ Remember that it may be best to avoid formal procedures, which can be stressful in themselves.
○ Don't answer threats with threats.
○ Ask colleagues to be supporting witnesses.
○ If the harassment occurs in written memoranda or instructions, keep dated copies and keep your dated reply to them.
○ If meetings take place to discuss the incidents insist on having a union representative or other professional colleague present. Following any such meeting, write your own summary of the meeting and send a copy to all parties.
○ If the incidents lead to absence or illness on your part, make a record in the school accident book and obtain DSS form B1 95 *Accident at Work – what to do about it.*

No bird soars too high if it soars with its own wings.

Ralph Waldo Emerson

Anti-bullying strategies

- Never ignore suspected bullying.
- Don't make premature assumptions.
- Listen carefully to all accounts – several pupils saying the same thing does not necessarily mean that they are telling the truth.
- Adopt a problem-solving approach that moves pupils on from justifying themselves.
- Follow up; repeatedly check bullying has not resumed.
- Make it clear that bullying will not be tolerated.
- Set in place a school anti-bullying strategy:
    - identify danger spots and safe areas around the site
    - raise awareness for the whole school community
    - introduce assertiveness training
    - reinforce good behaviour
    - listen to pupils' views
    - introduce peer support schemes
    - make it possible for pupils to report bullying incidents
    - introduce 'no blame' and 'shared concern' attitudes.

For more info visit www.dfes.gov.uk/bullying

Teaching is not a lost art, but the regard for it is a lost tradition.

Jacques Barzun

Surviving social occasions

Meeting colleagues in non-work situations can be difficult, as the day-to-day relationship has to be recreated. Teachers are infamous for talking about the classroom and curriculum even out of school, which is difficult for a non-teaching spouse.

○ Will there be parents or pupils watching you let your hair down?
○ Enter the room confidently, smile and keep a hand free to shake hands. Look around the room before deciding where to go.
○ Find out whether partners are welcome.
○ Wear something that is comfortable and which you feel confident in.
○ Start by approaching either a friendly face or someone you know rather than the most influential person. Later you may wish to broaden your range of friends.
○ Have in your mind a brief sound-bite about yourself, preferably one which describes you as more than just a teacher and which might be used as a 'hook' for others to ask questions about you.
○ Prepare icebreakers, about the place where this event is being held, the food, music, people and the journey to get there.
○ Ask about and be interested in, the people you are talking to. Ask about their connection with the host or the school and what particular project or topic are they working on at the moment?
○ Avoid complaining about the job or the people.
○ Watch body language. Other people looking over your shoulder or casting their eyes elsewhere are clear signs that it's time to move on.
○ Know your limits, especially if you need the support of a glass in your hand.
○ Plan your exit. Heads and deputies may recognize that a brief appearance is appreciated but they can become the ghost at the feast.

We worry about what a child will be tomorrow, yet we forget that he is someone today.   Stacia Tauscher

LIST 56 Recognizing drug abuse at school

If six of the following signs are present for a period of time, you should seek professional help.

Signs at school

- Sudden drop in grades, or truancy, or loss of interest in learning
- Sleeping in class
- Poor work performance and not doing homework
- Defiant of authority
- Poor attitude towards sports or other extracurricular activities
- Reduced memory and attention span
- Not informing parents of teacher meetings, open houses, etc.

Physical and emotional signs

- Changes friends
- Smell of alcohol or marijuana on breath or body
- Unexplainable mood swings and behaviour
- Negative, argumentative, paranoid or confused, destructive, anxious
- Over-reacts to criticism, acts rebellious
- Sharing few if any of their personal problems
- Doesn't seem as happy as they used to be
- Overly tired or hyperactive
- Drastic weight loss or gain
- Unhappy and depressed
- Cheats, steals
- Always needs money, or has excessive amounts of money
- Sloppy appearance
- Finding any of the following: cigarette rolling papers, pipes, roach clips, small glass vials, plastic baggies, remnants of drugs (seeds, etc.).

(From parentingteens.about.com)

Teachers who differentiate have at least two things in common: a conviction that students differ in their learning profiles, a belief that classrooms in which students are active learners are more effective.   Carol Tomlinson

Features that make a good library/resources centre

- Librarians who are knowledgeable, friendly, helpful, sociable, hardworking and cooperative.
- Funding which is adequate, consistent and in proportion to department capitation.
- Senior management team support and a line of communication that leads to and from the top.
- A building plan that places the library at the centre.
- A curriculum plan that places the library at the centre.
- A strict weeding policy producing up-to-date and relevant stock that looks good.
- A computerized catalogue.
- DVDs, CD-ROMs and processing software that is fun, informative and practical.
- Stock that matches curriculum needs and pupils' personal needs.
- Friendships with librarians and links connecting the librarians to departments and teachers.
- Projects that are resource based and are embedded in the curriculum.
- A methodical ICT skills policy which affects every pupil and teacher.
- A methodical information skills policy, which affects every pupil and teacher.

Some educators say a 'good' education is one that ensures that all students learn certain core information and master certain competencies.
Others define a 'good' education as one that helps students maximize their capacity as learners. Carol Tomlinson

LIST 58   Assemblies and collective worship

All maintained schools should provide for collective worship and religious education (RE) for their pupils.

- They must provide daily collective worship for pupils – except for those who have been withdrawn from this by their parents.
- If a parent asks for their child to be excused from RE or collective worship the school must comply.
- The school remains responsible for the supervision of any child withdrawn from RE or collective worship.
- Daily collective worship must be wholly or mainly of a broadly Christian character.
- If a broadly Christian act of worship is not suitable, the Standing Advisory Council on Religious Education (SACRE) can have the Christian content requirement lifted.
- Teachers cannot normally be required to lead or attend collective worship except in a religious designated school.

A regular assembly needs variety. Aim to change the speaker, message, and presentation method frequently. Use music, song, slides, an outside speaker, film clips . . . to avoid 'talking heads'.

Visit www.teachernet.gov.uk/teachingandlearning/assemblies/ for a variety of assembly ideas.

- Add items of topical interest whenever possible.
- Use topics and language accessible to the ability and age group of your audience.
- Capture and engage their attention.
- Be clear about the message you're trying to convey.
- Is the message understandable by this age group?
- Is the moral clear by the end of the assembly?
- Is it an issue which could be followed up by class teachers? If so, warn them beforehand.
- Ensure everyone can see and hear you and the presentation.
- Try to make the presentation memorable.
- Don't over-run into lesson time unless you have the cooperation of all teachers.
- If involving pupils themselves provide preparation time for them

and/or include this in lesson planning. Pupil presentations coming from curriculum activities can be very stimulating.

○ Create atmosphere for pupils entering and leaving the hall with appropriate music. This may relate to the message and should generally be calming rather than exciting.

○ Take the opportunity to identify the name of the music and its composer and performer.

○ Will pupils enter the hall silently or quietly? Make your expectations clear at the beginning of the year.

○ Consider whether to have a prayer or a few moments of silent reflection – and make this part of a recognizable routine.

○ Consider which messages might better be communicated in a printed bulletin and which will have more effect in an assembly.

○ Leave everyone feeling that it was a worthwhile event rather than a routine chore.

School is where you go between when your parents can't take you and industry can't take you.   John Updike

Games skills

A skill can be made easier or more difficult by adding one or more of the following features. Achieve differentiation by having small groups rehearsing a variety of skills according to ability. The example here is of catching, though these apply to all skills.

- Space: still or on the move (catching is easy when static, more difficult when moving).
- Distance: close together or far apart (close catching is easy; distance requires greater accuracy).
- Equipment: large, small, heavy or light (lightweight bats, short handles, medium balls).
- Direction: forwards, sideways, backwards (straightahead is easiest, twisting and turning raises the difficulty level).
- Level: high, medium, low (vary this in catching practice).
- Speed: quickly, slowly (add a time factor to increase difficulty).
- Force: hard, soft (it's more difficult to catch a forcefully struck ball).
- Body parts used: feet, one hand, two hands (increase coordination and difficulty by varying hands and feet).
- With others: partners, small groups (increases decisions and directions).
- Combination of skills: linking actions, stopping and starting (catch, turn and then throw).
- With opposition: decision making, being challenged for possession while adopting a series of skills.

A classroom is to education what a filing cabinet is to creativity. It boxes in, it cramps and confines, it limits where it should extend. It makes ideas into gobs of chewing gum.   Duncan Grey

Primary school swimming lessons

Introductory activities should be:

○ Active
○ Enjoyable
○ Help children get used to water temperature
○ Establish class control and organization
○ Establish concentration
○ Familiar yet interesting
○ Contrast with the main session

For beginners:

○ Hold the rail, jump up and down, shoulders under water.
○ Hold the rail, float on your back, beat legs up and down.
○ Jump away from the rail, keep arms outstretched for balance, turn and jump back to the rail.
○ Play follow my leader in twos and threes.

For non-beginners:

○ *Float and glide*: push off from the side on your front and glide. Note the distance travelled and try to increase the distance. Floating, rolling over back to front through horizontal and vertical axes.
○ *Underwater*: touch the bottom of the pool with your foot, hand, seat or knee. Swim through a hoop. Handstands. Pick up a rubber brick.
○ *Synchronized*: devise synchronized partner sequences.
○ *Endurance*: swim for 20 seconds without stopping. Swim a number of widths without stopping. Swim and rest, measure distance, time the rest.
○ *Speed*: time how many seconds to swim 'x' widths. Measure how far you can swim in 'x' seconds.
○ *Life saving*: life saving with a float. Practise life-saving kick (inverted breast stroke). Walk while towing a partner in a life-saving hold (under the chin).
○ *Competitive*: compete to find who can do 20 kicks fastest. Tread water for two minutes. Who is first to jump ten times and clap their hands under water ten times.

○ *Water polo*: pass a ball in small groups. Keep up the ball in the group without it touching the water. Swim to pick up the ball and throw back.

(From Hopper, B., Grey, J. and Maude, T. (2000) *Teaching Physical Education in the Primary School*. London: Routledge Falmer.)

Quality is never an accident; it is always the result of high intention, sincere effort, intelligent direction and skilful execution; it represents the wise choice of many alternatives. Willa A. Foster

The school drama production

Educational targets

○ Exploring, investigating and creating; communicating and presenting.

○ Offer pupils a variety of production tasks: acting and directing, set design and building, prop and costume research and making, scripting and make-up.

○ Offer a variety of management tasks: finance, advertising, sponsorship, assistant to director.

Before you start

○ Ensure support from musicians, set designers, technical assistants, lighting and sound engineers, dance coaches, teachers who may have their lessons disrupted, school managers who may have to back you up, parents who support their children's involvement.

○ Find other schools or groups who have staged the same or similar production and would loan costumes and props.

○ Create a detailed auditions and rehearsal schedule which fits into the school calendar, is publicized from the beginning (no excuses for skivers) and provides optional extra sessions in case of problems.

○ Book rehearsal and performance space. Large open areas like halls and drama studios are very desirable in schools and may be taken over for a variety of uses when you expected to be teaching drama. Watch out for PTA and public meetings of all kinds.

○ Ensure maintenance of existing equipment and hire of extra lighting, sound, costumes, props.

Production roles

○ Producer
○ Director
○ Assistant Director
○ Prompter
○ Scenic Designer
○ Technical Director
○ Stage Manager
○ Properties Chief

- Business Manager
- Publicity Manager
- House Manager

Some of these roles may be combined but all the jobs need to be done.

Don't forget

- Script and music copyright
- An agreed budget
- Adequate copies of the script
- Ticketing
- Publicity
- Sponsorship
- Recording a video and stills of the production
- Enlisting parents and teachers to help with costumes and props
- Booking the rehearsal and performance space
- Cover lessons for final rehearsals
- Thanks cards and presents for helpers
- Post-production party
- A break for yourself and your partner afterwards

The objective of education is to prepare the young to educate themselves throughout their lives. Robert Maynard Hutchins

Managing a school drama production

Golden rules of stage management

1. **Don't panic.** You above all must remain calm, cool and collected.
2. **Safety first.** Before and after every performance, clean the floor, secure flats, large props and platforms, check fire escapes are clear and lit. Check first-aid kits and fire extinguishers.
3. **Think ahead.** Plan to avoid problems. Have a comprehensive problem-solving kit, including gaffer tape.
4. **Be on time.** Be the first person in and the last person out of the theatre.
5. **Communicate.** Talk to everyone. Send a written note about any significant decision or arrangement. Make people happy by solving their problems, providing coffee and biscuits, hole punching all paperwork.

Director's script analysis

Divide the paper into columns from left to right:

○ Act/Scene/Page
○ Set
○ Lighting
○ Costumes/make-up
○ Props
○ Sound
○ Special effects

Make notes on any and every technical aspect of the production.
Read both dialogue and stage directions.

The prompt copy

Should include:

○ Cast list
○ Contact sheet
○ Rehearsal schedule
○ Attendance sheet
○ Conflict calendar
○ Emergency information

- Blocking key
- Pre-show
- Act I
- Intermission
- Act II
- Post-show details
- Cue sheets
- Rehearsal reports
- Performance reports
- Publicity
- Programme information
- Scenery
- Lighting
- Costumes, make-up and hair
- Properties
- Sound
- Performance schedules
- Scripts, sides and musical scores (numbered)

An education isn't how much you have committed to memory, or even how much you know. It's being able to differentiate between what you do know and what you don't. It's knowing where to go to find out what you need to know; and it's knowing how to use the information you get.

William Feather

Study support

Study support is a term covering a range of learning activities outside normal lessons which young people take part in voluntarily.

Its purpose is to improve young people's motivation, build their self-esteem and help them to become more effective learners. Above all, it aims to raise achievement.

> *'Success for young people also relies on the homework and self-directed learning that they do out of school hours, and classroom learning flourishes when good teaching and self-directed learning meet.'*
>
> John MacBeath, Professor of Education at Strathclyde University

Study support includes:

- ○ Homework clubs (facilities and support to do homework).
- ○ Help with key skills, including literacy, numeracy and ICT.
- ○ Study clubs (linked to or extending curriculum subjects).
- ○ Sports, games and adventurous outdoor activities.
- ○ Creative ventures (music, drama, dance, film and the full range of arts).
- ○ Residential events – study weeks or weekends.
- ○ Space and support for coursework and exam revision.
- ○ Opportunities for volunteering activities in the school or community.
- ○ Opportunities to pursue particular interests (science, ICT, law, archaeology, languages).
- ○ Mentoring by adults or other pupils.
- ○ Learning about learning (thinking skills, accelerated learning).
- ○ Community service (crime prevention initiatives, environmental clubs).

(From 'Extending Opportunity: A National Framework for Study Support', DfES 1998.)

I am always eager to learn, but I do not always like being taught.
Winston Churchill

ICT | 6

LIST 64 — Why have a school website?

How can a website serve our school?

- The *worst* reason is because the head wants 'http://www.ourschool.html' on the school letterhead.
- The *best* reason is to enhance the curriculum and inform the school community.
- Advertise your institution; show pupils' work to the world.
- Stimulate students' learning, provide a forum and a purpose for school work.

The website as a resource

- Makes school-generated curriculum materials accessible to pupils at home as well as at school.
- Provide selected relevant and useful websites.

The website as an instructional tool   Provide source material for information handling – evaluation of existing materials and resources, selecting and balancing different information, creating new materials for different audiences from a variety of sources – without resorting to plagiarism – then presenting them on the school's website for others to use.

A worldwide audience for your students

- A stimulus and a purpose for English lessons and a partner for experiments.
- Share weather statistics between continents.

The community

- Information for parents, ex-pupils and local people, including parents of future pupils and a repository of homework and school news.

To teach is to learn twice.   Joseph Joubert

School website design

General

○ Attractive and in a style that suits the school's image and the site's content.

○ Design templates using these features in a range of ways, so that you both offer help and maintain a standard.

○ Use background pattern and text colour to make reading easy.

○ Email address of person responsible should appear on every page – or a central address if you are concerned about giving our students' email addresses.

○ Every page should have a link to at least one other page on the site and always back to the main school home page.

Graphics

○ Graphics should be used where they add to the page, but do not detract from content.

○ Graphics should load quickly (always test online in actual conditions).

○ Link graphics should be accompanied by text links.

○ Avoid flashing images!

Sound and movies

○ Sound and movie files should load at the request of the user.

○ Sounds/movies should be less than 500 kb or should be streamed so that the user doesn't have to wait for the full download before viewing or listening.

Give a person a fish and you will feed them for a day: Teach them to fish and you feed them for a lifetime.   Chinese Proverb

School website interface and navigation design

These don't just look pretty or grab attention, they also help a user to navigate easily around the site.

- ○ Keep the interface simple.
- ○ Keep the information load low.
- ○ Avoid great contrasts in colours.
- ○ Maximize legibility.
- ○ Make navigation consistent (style, position).
- ○ Use metaphors and icons to make things familiar.
- ○ Offer a variety of guided tours, alternative routes around your site.
- ○ Test your pages on a variety of users – and act on their criticisms!
- ○ Choose a reading level appropriate to your audience.
- ○ Choose graphics appropriate to your audience.
- ○ Give your layout a structure.
- ○ Divide text into logical chunks.
- ○ Be wary of changing the colour of hypertext links.
- ○ Avoid jargon, slang or 'inappropriate language'.
- ○ Test out the pages on:
  - – PCs and Macs
  - – colour-blind users
  - – different browsers
  - – different screen sizes.
- ○ Make clear links from the home page to each area of your site.
- ○ Make a link back to the home page from all pages.

The highest result of education is tolerance.   Helen Keller

School website content

General information

○ About your school for the general public (future parents).
○ For local authority, government education department, governors.
○ For parents, both present and future.
○ For teachers both at the school and other schools.
○ For students at the school.
○ For your feeder schools or partner schools.
○ Refer to content's original source and/or hypertext linked.
○ Keep the information up-to-date and show this with 'updated'.

About the school

○ Where it is, what size, general information. Include address and map.
○ School policies, especially Internet/computer use policies.
○ Calendar of events and relevant staff names/email addresses.
○ Homework assignments and deadlines.

For parents

○ School rules and philosophy.
○ Links to appropriate education sites and general interest sites appropriate to parents.
○ Advice on Internet matters (where to place your home computer, how you can help improve your child's ICT skills).

For teachers

○ Professional development links.
○ Lesson plans and sites of interest.
○ Departmental plans and curricular material.
○ Feeder school and partner school contact details.

For students

○ Links for students at all levels.

Careers information

○ Information about courses provided in the school and elsewhere.
○ Student-created work, pages, sites and homework.

By learning you will teach; by teaching you will learn.   Latin Proverb

Staff intranet content

- Ask staff what they want.
- Emphasize that an intranet is not for open viewing. It is designed to be limited to access by staff only.
- You may choose whether site managers, cleaners, support staff, etc. need access to teacher areas.
- Access must be password protected to prevent pupil access.
- Pupils may, of course, have their own intranet.
- Make this site a one-stop shop for all professional information.
- Include school documents, ensuring that the latest version is always online:
  - Staff handbook
  - School calendar
  - Staff list, with names, initials, subjects taught, responsibilities
  - School phone numbers
  - Curriculum and policy documents
  - Medical and emergency procedures
  - Minutes of meetings.
- Student data and access to the school management system (bearing in mind the Data Protection Act).
- Links to local authority documents.
- Lists of local authority contacts and agencies.
- Trade unions' websites and local reps.
- Links to national documents and to national educational portals:
  - Curriculum Online
  - National Grid for Learning
  - Department for Education
  - Teachers' pensions
  - Teachernet
  - Teacher Training Agency.

Consensus is the absence of principle and an abundance of expediency.
Margaret Thatcher

Internet safety for pupils

Acceptable use guidelines

All pupils must conform to current school rules in terms of acceptable behaviour, use of school facilities, etc.

- Behaviour on the network must be in support of education and research and consistent with the educational objectives of the school and these guidelines.
- You are responsible for what you say and do while using the network. Because communication with thousands of others is so quick and easy, it is important for you to think before speaking and to show respect for other people and for their ideas.
- Do not attempt to pass off Internet information as your own. Respect copyright and ownership at all times.
- You are responsible for the security of your password. You must keep it secret.
- When searching for material on the Internet, ask yourself, 'Would I be happy to show this to my teacher or parent?'. If the answer is no, you should not be looking at that material. Move on to a more suitable page immediately.
- You must always be able to give a satisfactory educational reason to a teacher for your use of the network and the Internet in particular.
- The use of the network is a privilege, not a right.
- Inappropriate use will mean loss of access.

Culture is a treasure which follows its owner everywhere. Chinese Proverb

- Think carefully before sending a message.
- Include your name and school on email messages – but remember that you represent the school and its reputation.
- Don't give your home address or phone number, or post those of students or colleagues.
- Check email frequently.
- Be careful with sarcasm and humour; your 'joke' may be misinterpreted.
- Don't be vulgar or offensive or swear in your messages.
- Don't publicly criticize or anger others.
- When quoting in a message, give its author or source.
- Use all capitals only to highlight a word; capitals are email shouting.
- Make your subject line descriptive, yet short.
- Don't send personal messages to group lists, or newsgroups.
- Selectively quote any question you are answering.
- When posting a question to a discussion group, request that replies be sent to you personally as email, not to the entire list. You may wish to summarize all replies later and forward the summary to the list as a 'hit'.

Everything government touches turns to lead.   Randall Terry

Top ICT teaching tips

○ Every pupil should sign-up to an Acceptable Use Policy (AUP).

○ Always have a backup plan involving no computers.

○ Have alternative work for those who have forgotten their password.

○ Have alternative work for those attempting to browse unsuitable sites, who send rude email messages, or who otherwise break their agreement to the AUP. This will probably include copying out the AUP and having their password withdrawn.

○ Pupils who are not reliable users but who may need computer access should have a password known only to the teacher and entered by the teacher each session.

○ Tell pupils to remember their passwords using an acronym of words and numbers (minimum six characters) which recalls a favourite song or saying e.g. 'I'll be true to you for ever' becomes IBT2U4E.

○ Publish your lesson plans and activities on the school intranet and/ or website. Your work is therefore prepared in advance, ready for any absence and available to absent pupils if need be.

○ Prepare an email address group for each class so that you can send them instructions, advice, collect responses, give and collect homework, etc.

○ Stick to a seating plan so you can track any damage, lost mouse balls, origin of inappropriate messages, etc.

○ Provide a program guide for each of the main applications you expect to use. Tell pupils to try using the guide before asking you.

○ Emphasize the essential need for everyone to save their work. Save it – save it again.

Get your facts first, and then you can distort 'em as much as you please.
Mark Twain

Website guidelines

○ The school website will conform to the aims in the Acceptable Use Guidelines.

○ The school website will conform to the normal school rules.

○ The school website will conform to the use of appropriate language and behaviour.

○ Remember that the website presents the face of the school to the world. We insist on high standards of content, accuracy and presentation.

○ All information published on the website must be checked by the webmaster.

○ Photographs and pupil details should be used carefully to avoid identification from outside the school community. Prefer group pictures and first name only.

○ Respect copyright and ownership.

○ Avoid links to any external sites which might cause embarrassment.

○ Include a statement denying responsibility of any external links.

○ Include a link to the webmaster's address to report any glitches, errors and links.

My plan is to end all plans. The country has been planned to death.

Will Rogers

Never trust computers: contingency plans

You must *always* have a backup plan. What would you do if there was an Ofsted inspector in the room? You'd force yourself to keep calm, take over the class and actively teach the class something. You wouldn't dive under the desk to pull out cables, restart more than four times, phone the technician and then go looking for her while the class went wild . . .

So . . .

○ Assume that there will be a problem and plan to overcome it.
○ Keep a list of ICT-related topics, quotations and news clippings and be prepared to have a discussion about them. For example:
  – What would we do if all the computers in the world caught a bug and died?
  – How could we avoid or minimize that scenario?
  – Anyone can make a mistake – but it takes a computer to really mess things up.
  – 'There will come a time when the computers will control the people.' Is it possible? Has it started already? How might we stop it?
  – A cyborg is part man, part machine. We are already developing implants which enhance people's powers. Where will it end?
○ Have paper available (used print-out paper is ideal) and give ICT-related written or graphic tasks.
○ Use a whiteboard or flip chart instead of the big screen or data projector.
○ Keep a set of text books with a range of tasks.
○ Display interesting and informative ICT-related posters to use as learning materials.
○ Teach the unavoidable fact that we cannot afford to rely on computers in our lives – there are always alternatives.

Ah consensus . . . the process of abandoning all beliefs, principles, values and policies in search of something in which no one believes, but to which no one objects . . .   Margaret Thatcher

ICT-related written or graphic tasks

○ Design a website on paper to reflect your personality, friends and lifestyle.

○ Design a website for your year group, including recreational and academic links.

○ Recreate the school website in the playground using members of your class as the pages and chalk marks or string to show the links between them.

○ Back in the classroom commit this to paper by quizzing each class member and writing down what they say should appear on each page. Later this could be built into a real website.

○ Design unambiguous symbols to reflect your personality and interests. Test for clarity with other people in your class.

○ Write a diary or blog for a day listing and describing the influence ICT has on it.

At home

TV news delivery, mail sorted by them, bills calculated, newspapers designed and printed, personal email collected, homework written.

At school

letters home, grades calculated, records kept, learning materials produced, timetables designed, library catalogue stored, school website produced;

While shopping

bills, stock control, publicity, consumer information collated, credit card debited and calculated.

I was to learn later in life that we tend to meet any new situation by reorganizing and a wonderful method it can be for creating the illusion of progress (change), while producing confusion, inefficiency, and demoralization. Pretonius Arbiter-Chief Lt of the Emperor Nero

Checklists for website evaluation

Authority and accuracy

○ Is it a hoax, or genuine research? (Look at the site address, URL.)
○ Do you know anything about the author? (Title – Prof., Dr or description – head of department.)
○ Is there a name and contact address?
○ Obvious errors (typography, spelling errors, inappropriate language and pictures, a mistaken sense of humour).
○ Supportive evidence? (Can you cross-check facts with other sources of information? Look for published references and dates.)

Opinion and objectivity

○ Is it fact or opinion? (Look for bias and prejudice.)
○ Is it a commercial, governmental, personal or academic website?
○ Who is sponsoring the page or the site?
○ What kind of commercial banner advertisements do they feature?
○ What is the purpose of the page? (Is it to inform, persuade, sell, explain?)
○ Which country does it come from? (Some countries are less tolerant than others about social and religious matters.)

Currency and coverage

○ Is it up-to-date and well maintained?
○ Does it look at all sides of the issue?
○ Are the site's links to other sites inappropriate or broken?
○ Does it tell you more than, or better than, you could find out elsewhere?

Ah consensus ... the process of avoiding the very issues that have to be solved, merely because you cannot get agreement on the way ahead.
Margaret Thatcher

LIST 76

Educational websites

- TeacherNet (USA): teachers.net
- TeacherNet UK Gov: www.teachernet.gov.uk
- Association of Teachers' Websites: www.byteachers.org.uk
- UK National Grid for Learning: www.ngfl.gov.uk
- Virtual Teachers' Centre: www.vtc.ngfl.gov.uk
- National Curriculum Online: www.nc.uk.net/home.html
- UK Department for Education and Skills: www.dfes.gov.uk/index.html
- Learn co.uk: www.learn.co.uk
- Times Educational: www.tes.co.uk
- Curriculum Online: www.curriculumonline.gov.uk
- BECTa: www.becta.org.uk
- EduWeb: www.eduweb.co.uk
- BBC Web Guide: www.bbc.co.uk/webguide/schools/index.shtml
- Education.com: uk.education.com

I have come to a frightening conclusion. I am the decisive element in the classroom. It is my personal approach that creates the climate. It is my daily mood that makes the weather. As a teacher I possess tremendous power to make a child's life miserable or joyous. I can be a tool of torture or an instrument of inspiration. I can humiliate or humour, hurt or heal. In all situations it is my response that decides whether crisis will be escalated or de-escalated and a child humanized or de-humanized. Dr Hiam Ginott

Bureaucracy and Management | 7

 LIST 77 **Holding a meeting**

Meetings can be for discussion, updating, getting to know people or making decisions. They are notoriously bad at most of these things, though without them people can feel disenfranchized.

○ Updating is better done on paper or by email.
○ Never read out a report at a meeting.
○ Provide printed materials well in advance.
○ Don't hold formal meetings to generate good ideas – arrange relaxed brainstorming sessions instead.
○ Consider who should attend. Appoint people to represent the views of others. Be clear about why each person is there.
○ Arrange targeted small sub-committees for specialist topics.
○ Calendar meetings in advance.
○ Consider whether a brief stand-up meeting at break might replace a long sit-down session after school.
○ Ask participants what they think is important for discussion. Get feedback from the participants.
○ Publish the agenda in advance to help members prepare.
○ Arrange the agenda in order of importance. Notify AOB (any other business) in advance of the start of the meeting.
○ If tending to over-run (e.g. over an hour) consider setting a guillotine on individual items.
○ Make the minutes widely available.
○ What happens when a committee makes a decision? Does it have the power to carry out its decisions or are they referred on – and lost? Consider disbanding if you are unable to achieve anything.

Education without religion, useful as it is, seems rather to make man a more clever devil. C. S. Lewis

Essential phrases for report writing

Accuracy   Exact, precise, meticulous; not always . . ., generally . . ., should aim for a higher rate of . . ., hasty, careless.

Enthusiasm   Great, considerable, infectious, overwhelming, receptive, responsive, inventive, spontaneous; lack of, unresponsive.

Motivation   Shows great . . ., enthusiastic, determined; lacks . . ., misplaced . . .

Work effort   Diligent, hard working, always gives his/her best, industrious, methodical, painstaking, persistent, systematic, single-minded, thorough; easily distracted, does not give of his/her best, laborious, worthy, idle, slow, spasmodic.

Reliability   Entirely reliable, trustworthy, has high standards, can always be relied on to . . ., cannot be relied on to . . .

Ability   Able, considerable, some, subtle, talented, shows signs of . . ., exceptional, inspired, bright, capable, perceptive, flair, aware, competent; lack of, confused, lacks basic skills, finds difficulty in understanding, over-estimates his/her own . . ., unrealistic about his/her own . . ., vague, limited.

Progress   Has made steady, high achiever, improving, making headway, turned over a new leaf, significant . . .; steady . . .; declining, slipping back, has made little . . ., should aim to make more . . ., struggling.

Potential   Has, successful, considerable, making, has the potential to become . . .; has not shown his/her real . . ., has not lived up to . . ., making slow . . .

Behaviour   Responsive, alert, sensible, polite, well-mannered, obedient, respectful, cooperative, lively; challenging, aggressive, undisciplined, attention seeking, disturbing, distracting, disrespectful, destructive, anti-social, unreasonable, demands an audience, troublesome, irresponsible.

Character   Has initiative, enthusiastic, reliability, honesty, imagination, charming, sensitive, cheerful, happy, confident, self-possessed, a delightful student; apathetic, impatient, impetuous, indecisive, irresponsible, resentful, unresponsive, aggressive, untrustworthy, withdrawn, earnest, hostile, ungrateful.

Presentation　Impeccable, attractive, thoughtful, neat, painstaking, precise, detailed, imaginative; needs to consider, lacks the skills.

Attendance　Regular, reliable; infrequent, irregular; lack of . . ., hinders progress, more frequent . . . would . . .

Cooperation　Always helpful, works well in groups, responsive, contributes well, participates in . . ., helps others; challenging, antagonistic, selfish.

Social skills　Polite, shows respect for others, willing to help others, a good listener, a good leader, responsive, mature.

Attainment　Higher/lower/appropriate (for this stage/class/level); high, excellent, lower than potential, limited by (behaviour, attitude, attendance . . .).

Preferred learning styles　Cooperating with others, independent, practical, written, oral, active; too often depends on others, needs to develop a wider range of . . .

There is no sure cure so idiotic that some superintendent of schools will not swallow it.　　　　　　　　　　　　　　　H. L. Mencken

More phrases for report writing

All purpose phrases for colourless or forgotten students

- ○ Has potential for improvement.
- ○ Satisfactory, competent, acceptable, moderate, limited.
- ○ Needs to be thorough in his/her approach to written work.
- ○ Has maintained a reasonable standard.
- ○ Adequate, fair.

Words and phrases to avoid   Thick, dull, dim, dim-witted, witless, slow-witted, backward, retarded, stupid, handicapped, docile, liar, thief, devious, a fool.

Euphemisms   Prefer 'unacceptable' and 'inappropriate' to 'awful', 'dreadful', 'appalling', 'disgraceful'.

In general

- ○ Refer to achievement and to provable or quantifiable behaviour rather than character and personality.
- ○ Be specific rather than generalize.
- ○ Be temperate rather than emotional.
- ○ Provide suggestions for improvement or redemption rather than general criticism.

From cradle to grave this problem of running order through chaos, direction through space, discipline through freedom, unity through multiplicity, has always been, and must always be, the task of education.

Henry Brooks Adams

What we really mean when we say . . .

- Satisfactory progress – Who is this child? I can't think of anything to say about him/her.
- A born leader – A threatening bully.
- Easy going – Utterly idle.
- Lively – Disruptive and violent.
- Good progress – If you think his/her work is bad now, you should have seen it at the start of term!
- Helpful – Creep.
- Reliable – Grasses on his/her mates.
- Has difficulty in forming stable relationships – Deeply unpleasant.
- Easily distracted – Has done no work at all.
- Expresses himself/herself confidently – Cheeky little so-and-so.
- Imaginative – Lies and cheats at all times.
- Does not accept authority easily – Constantly excluded.
- Better at practical activities – Illiterate.
- Doing exceptionally well, a delightful child – Mother is Chair of Governors.
- Often appears tired – On the game or glue sniffing till dawn.
- Good with his/her hands – Thief.
- Inclined to daydream – Seriously dim.

Nothing in education is so astonishing as the amount of ignorance it accumulates in the form of inert facts.   Henry Brooks Adams

- 'Certainly on the road to failure' on John Lennon.
- 'She must try to be less emotional in her dealings with others' on Diana, Princess of Wales.
- 'He cannot be trusted to behave himself anywhere' on Winston Churchill.
- 'He shows great originality, which must be curbed at all costs' on Peter Ustinov.
- 'As a pupil she is very satisfactory, but even that is of small account when you compare it with the perfect quality of her soul' on Eleanor Roosevelt.
- 'He confesses he will not make a biologist – and I am inclined to agree with him' on Duncan Grey.
- 'Diana has been very tiresome in the dormitory this term' on Diana Rigg.
- 'He would much sooner write an intimate memoir of Julius Caesar than a factual account of his Gallic wars. But then, who wouldn't? Unfortunately examiners demand fact' on Bruce Chatwin.
- 'It would seem that Briers thinks he is running the school and not me. If this attitude persists one of us will have to leave' on Richard Briers.
- 'He is extremely sensitive to the wrongs and injustices of the world as he sees them . . .' on Dennis Potter.
- 'Scored average for most things, including intelligence' on George Bush.
- Take comfort from a speech George W. Bush made to Yale graduates:
  'To those of you who received honours, awards and distinctions, I say, well done. And to the C students, I say, you too can be President of the United States.'

(More examples in *Could Do Better*, edited by Catherine Hurley, 2002, Simon & Schuster, London.)

. . . be intolerant of ignorance, but understanding of illiteracy.

Maya Angelou

Useful phrases for references

Actual quotes from Federal employee performance evaluations.

- ○ 'Since my last report, he has reached rock bottom and has started to dig.'
- ○ 'His department would follow him anywhere, but only out of morbid curiosity.'
- ○ 'This employee is really not so much of a has-been, but more of a definitely won't be.'
- ○ 'Works well when under constant supervision and cornered like a rat in a trap.'
- ○ 'When she opens her mouth, it seems that this is only to change whichever foot was previously in there.'
- ○ 'He would be out of his depth in a parking lot puddle.'
- ○ 'This young lady has delusions of adequacy.'
- ○ 'She sets low personal standards and then consistently fails to achieve them.'
- ○ 'This employee should go far – and the sooner he starts, the better.'
- ○ 'The only time I have seen him at full stretch is on the football field.'
- ○ 'If you are thinking of giving this man a berth, make sure it's a wide one.'

Education is an ornament in prosperity, and a refuge in adversity. Aristotle

How to respond to the press

○ The number one rule is not to be rushed into responding to something without knowing the full story.

○ A question may be put to you in such a way that there is presumption of responsibility or guilt by the school or its members. Don't in any way agree to this. Don't say 'no comment', but as courteously and professionally as possible do not comment.

○ Buy time by saying that you will ask the people involved, consult colleagues and governors and get back to the questioner when the facts are clear. Don't make snap judgements.

○ Do consult colleagues and anyone involved in the situation. Do refer to the chair of governors and to any press official in the LEA.

○ If the situation looks as if it might be bad publicity for the school, find appropriate examples which show the school in a better light – its past unblemished record, its well known policies on the subject, its caring ethos, its popularity, etc.

○ Don't sweep the issue under the carpet, don't diminish its importance, but do strive to place it in context. A considered press statement is probably less risky than a spontaneous address at the school gates.

○ With photographers, try to keep a serious demeanour for a serious issue. A laugh, smile or smirk at any time in the photo session could be used against you.

○ If bad publicity does come out, consider sending out a further press statement and a letter to parents, supported by governors and parents' association.

Education is the best provision for old age.   Aristotle

What the head really means to say

○ I thrive on challenge – I know you all hate me.

○ I am grateful for all the responses staff have sent me – I've filed the abusive letters to use against you in the future.

○ We shall create a working party – I'll make sure nothing actually happens.

○ I shall consult with the senior management team – I don't know what to do.

○ We must all pull together and we have hard decisions to make – You'd better get on with it, it's going to be hell.

○ I am in consultation with the chair of governors – I've managed to fool her so far; I think I'm about to get sacked, so I'm going to try to pin the blame on her.

○ I'd like to wish you all a happy Christmas – Oh no I wouldn't. Go home. Leave me alone.

○ I'd particularly like to think the support staff for their hard work – You're cheap and I'm amazed at how willing you still are.

○ I'd like to congratulate Mr Grey on his retirement – Thank god the old cynic has gone at last and freed up vital management points.

○ Fair funding – Unfair funding.

○ Inclusion – Exclusion.

○ Shrink, contract – euphemisms for fewer teachers, bigger classes.

○ This is a bold and courageous strategy – I know it's going to be painful and it's crazy. It's a blind reaction forced upon me by government cost cutting and by my previous strategies.

○ I have experience of managing difficult situations – I actually create them on a regular basis.

○ It is not that I am not an ideas man . . . – I just have no idea of quite how bad this is getting.

In educating the young we use pleasure and pain as rudders to steer their course.   Aristotle

Paper and email management

- Brief because brief is better.
- Deal with each piece as soon as possible.
- Make one of four choices for each item:
  1 Act on it.
  2 Pass it on to someone else to act on it.
  3 File it.
  4 Bin it.
- Tend to prefer the last of these four.
- Try to deal with each item only once.
- Ask yourself what is the worst that could happen if I throw this away?
- Just do it!
- Have a 'clear your desk day' on the first day of the holiday.
- Push for people to use email instead of paper.
- While email itself can become a problem it nevertheless can be:
  - deleted quickly
  - saved and filed easily
  - retrieved using a search or find facility
  - stored without a filing cabinet.
- If storage is an issue, a scanner with optical character recognition (OCR) can even turn a paper document into an electronic file with some degree of success.

Educated men are as much superior to uneducated men as the living are to the dead.   Aristotle

Excessive workload

The following activities have been agreed by the DfES and the teacher unions as 'common tasks' which 'need not routinely be carried out by teachers and should be transferred to support staff'.

- Collecting money
- Collating pupil reports
- Stocktaking
- Chasing absences
- Administering work experience
- Cataloguing, preparing, issuing and maintaining equipment and materials
- Bulk photocopying
- Administering examinations
- Minuting meetings
- Copy typing
- Invigilating examinations
- Coordinating and submitting bids
- Producing class lists
- Administering teacher cover
- Seeking and giving personnel advice
- Record keeping and filing
- ICT trouble-shooting and minor repairs
- Managing pupil data
- Classroom display
- Commissioning new ICT equipment
- Inputting pupil data
- Analysing attendance figures
- Ordering supplies and equipment
- Processing exam results
- Producing standard letters.

Knowledge is power.   Francis Bacon

Health and safety policy

The Health and Safety at Work Act of 1974 describes the responsibilities of employers. This legislation is enforced by the Health and Safety Executive (HSE).

A School Health and Safety Policy will include the following key elements:

○ A general statement of policy.
○ Delegation of duties as allocated tasks.
○ Arrangements made to put in place, monitor and review measures necessary to reach satisfactory health and safety standards.
○ Training of staff in health and safety, including competence in risk assessment.
○ Off-site visits including school-led adventure activities.
○ Selecting and controlling contractors.
○ First-aid and supporting pupils' medical needs.
○ School security.
○ Occupational health services and work-related stress.
○ Consultation arrangements with employees.
○ Workplace safety for teachers, pupils and visitors.
○ Violence to staff.
○ Manual handling.
○ Slips and trips.
○ On-site vehicle movements.
○ Management of asbestos.
○ Control of hazardous substances.
○ Maintenance and, when necessary, examinations and tests of equipment such as electrical equipment, local exhaust ventilation, pressure systems, gas appliances, lifting equipment and glazing safety.
○ Recording and reporting accidents to staff, pupils and visitors, including those reportable under the Reporting of Injuries, Diseases and Dangerous Occurrences Regulations 1995 (RIDDOR).
○ Fire safety, including testing of alarms and evacuation procedures.
○ Dealing with health and safety emergencies – procedures and contacts.

(From www.teachernet.gov.uk/)

Do not train youth to learn by harshness, but lead them to it by what amuses their minds. Then you may discover the peculiar bent of the genius of each.   Plato

Assessment

Assessment includes:

- All classroom information about pupils
- Formal examinations
- Informal tests
- Essays
- Projects
- Classwork
- Homework
- Activities
- Performance in a variety of conditions
- Role-plays
- Discussions
- Portfolios of collected work, including drafts, to show process and development

Testing

- Offer tests which measure a range of learning goals – not only factual knowledge but thinking skills too.
- Offer tests using a method which suits learning goals – multiple choice, open essay, performance or activity.
- Tell the pupils what you expect of them, what you will be assessing and what you will not.
- Provide students with feedback and positive criticism.
- Provide students with a checklist of what was achieved and what was not.
- Integrate assessment tasks into lessons.
- Create tests which are structured and standardized so all pupils know the evaluation is fair.

The work can wait while you show the child the rainbow, but the rainbow won't wait while you do the work.   Patricia Clafford

National curriculum attainment targets at word level

An analysis of the vocabulary frequency of National Curriculum Targets.

KS3 English

- ○ Words which appear once: whereby, world, wildlife, whom, weave, unconventional, thou, once, simulated, jokes, Goldilocks, correct, bus-stop, mathematics, grammar.
- ○ Words which don't appear at all: stimulated, kids, enjoy, love, fun, excitement, lively, enthusiasm.
- ○ Other words: example/examples × 126; story/stories × 50; think × 2; teacher × 10; pupil(s) × 19.

KS3 Mathematics

- ○ Words which appear once: arbitrarily, digit, gallons, isosceles, thinking, obeys, obtuse, obvious, odd, one-thousandths, SAS, stem-and-leaf, pie, pints.
- ○ Words which don't appear at all: enjoy, love, fun, excitement, lively, enthusiasm.
- ○ Other words: '+' × 27; algebra/ic × 19; arithmetic × 2; cuboids × 4; decomposition × 2; discounts × 2; example × 41; fraction(s) × 27; language × 2; negative × 7; not × 8; number(s) × 33; problem(s) × 48; simple × 16.

KS3 Science

- ○ Words which appear once: toxic, taxonomic, superglue, snowboards, questions, flowering, ear, deafness, cytoplasm, antagonistic, alcohol.
- ○ Words which don't appear at all: birth, creation, sex, enjoy, love, fun, excitement, lively, enthusiasm.
- ○ Other words: should × 23; not × 2; evidence × 15; language × 4; cannot × 2; life × 5.

Very small children are not susceptible to reason and should be taught by fear and awe.   John Locke, *Some Thoughts Concerning Education*, 1693

General Teaching

LIST 90   You must be in education if . . .

- You want to biff the next person who says 'It must be great to work from 9 to 4 and have such long holidays'.
- You want to biff the next teacher who says 'But he's no problem for me'.
- You find yourself waving a finger at children who misbehave in public.
- You don't have a life from September to July.
- You can't find a name for your own child because they all remind you of someone you've taught.
- You go to parties, latch on to other teachers and grumble about the latest initiatives.
- You go to parties and argue fiercely against any non-teacher who has a view on education.
- You collect bits of cartons, tin foil, shells, sweet wrappers and pinecones, because you know you can use them for display work next term.
- You mark and cut out articles in papers and magazines for use in next term's lessons.
- You want to get out.

I would live to study, and not study to live.   Francis Bacon

National Curriculum targets

English 1. Speaking and listening; 2. Reading; 3. Writing.

Maths 1. Using and applying mathematics; 2. Number and algebra; 3. Shape, space and measures; 4. Handling data.

Science 1. Scientific enquiry; 2. Life processes and living things; 3. Materials and their properties; 4. Physical processes.

Design and Technology Developing, planning and communicating ideas; working with tools, equipment, materials and components; evaluating processes and products; knowledge and understanding of materials and components, and systems and control structures.

Information and Communication Technology Finding things out; developing ideas and making things happen; exchanging and sharing information; reviewing modifying and evaluating work in progress.

History Chronological understanding; knowledge and understanding of events, people and changes in the past; historical interpretation; historical enquiry; organization and communication.

Geography Geographical enquiry and skills; knowledge and understanding of places; knowledge and understanding of patterns and processes; knowledge and understanding of environmental change and sustainable development.

Modern Foreign Languages 1. Listening and responding; 2. Speaking; 3. Reading and responding; 4. Writing.

Art and Design Exploring and developing ideas; investigating and making; evaluating and developing further work; knowledge and understanding.

Music Controlling sounds through singing and playing; creating and developing musical ideas; responding and reviewing; listening, and applying knowledge and understanding.

Physical Education Acquiring and developing skills; selecting and applying skills; evaluating and improving performance; knowledge and understanding of fitness and health.

Citizenship Knowledge and understanding about becoming informed citizens; developing skills of enquiry and communication; developing skills of participation and responsible action.

Education makes a people easy to lead, but difficult to drive; easy to govern, but impossible to enslave.   Lord Brougham

Unavoidable differences between boys and girls

○ Unskilled manual jobs which once went to boys no longer exist.
○ Girls outperform boys by ten per cent at five A to C grade GCSEs.
○ Seventy-five per cent of offences by 11- to 17-year-olds were committed by boys.
○ Boys are four times more likely to be addicted to drugs.
○ Boys are five times more likely to commit suicide.
○ Boys have poorer language skills at an early age.

Girls

○ Mature earlier.
○ Take school work more seriously and cooperate more.
○ Question less.
○ Appreciate situations and feelings more.
○ Persevere.

Boys

○ Acknowledge finer feelings less.
○ Are more sceptical and questioning.
○ Are less cooperative.
○ Are more susceptible to peer group pressure.
○ Read less.
○ Are more physically active.
○ Have less self-esteem on entering secondary school.

Teachers and parents

○ Praise female traits and control disaffected boys.
○ Value written work more than oral work.
○ Shout at boys, reason with girls.

Democracy means government by the uneducated, while aristocracy means government by the badly educated. G. K. Chesterton

LIST 93

Encouraging the boys

(Some of these points apply to girls too . . .)

- Behaviour: rules should be clear and consistent.
- Responsibilities: use boys as helpers, give them a role, a responsibility and a purpose.
- Structure lessons into short sections.
- Set short-term achievable targets.
- Use word frames and structured tasks within research tasks.
- Give lots of positive practical feedback and encouragement on how to improve.
- Actively seek to encourage – recognizing that praise in front of the class may be seen as embarrassing.
- Make lessons varied and active.
- Use a wide variety of learning styles with emphasis on physical, spatial and ICT-based work.
- Target suitable materials in the library/resources centre. Provide a list of fiction for boys and promote non-fiction reading too. Use non-fiction texts in the English classroom.
- Consider male oriented topics for research projects. Skateboarding and football are acceptable topics if the real education is in the act of research or writing.
- Boy-girl seating arrangements can help focused work.
- Invite suitable male role models as guests to school. Have successful male sixth formers take part in activities.
- Encourage dads to take an interest in projects (set them homework too!) and attend parents' evenings.
- Recognize that boys' standards of handwriting and presentation are frequently low. It is usually unhelpful to criticize this, though ICT may provide an answer.

Children who are treated as if they are uneducable almost invariably become uneducable. Kenneth B. Clark

Negotiating the English language minefield

Beware when writing or speaking for public consumption – pupil reports can be a minefield.

- ○ 'I' or 'me' as subject or object (you and I or you and me)?
- ○ Pronunciation emphasis (controversy, research).
- ○ Singularity or plurality (none is or none are)?
- ○ Adoption of American vocabulary and idioms (movies, fries).
- ○ Pronunciation of foreign words (restaurant).
- ○ Acceptability of regional pronunciations.
- ○ Split infinitives (to boldly go).
- ○ Different to or different from?
- ○ 'I wish I was' or 'I wish I were'?
- ○ Clichés.
- ○ Pronunciation which does not conform to spelling (Antarctic, library, secretary).
- ○ Confusables (uninterested/disinterested).
- ○ Ending a sentence with a preposition.
- ○ Who or whom?
- ○ Colloquial speech.
- ○ Euphemisms.
- ○ Pronunciation of 'r' sound where followed by a vowel (awe-inspiring, law-abiding but pouring).
- ○ Shall or will, should and would?
- ○ Pronunciation precision (last year, tissues, February).

Children have to be educated, but they have also to be left to educate themselves.   Abbe Dimnet

Useful Latin phrases

In the classroom

Die dulci fruere – Have a nice day.

Fac ut gaudeam – Make my day.

Trying for promotion

Si hoc signum legere potes, operis boni in rebus Latinus alacribus et fructuosis potiri potes! – If you can read this sign, you can get a good job in the fast-paced, high-paying world of Latin!

Noli me vocare, ego te vocabo – Don't call me, I'll call you.

In the staffroom

Ne auderis delere orbem rigidum meum! – Don't you dare erase my hard disk!

On the sports field

Gramen artificiosum od – I hate astroturf.

The headmaster

Sentio aliquos togatos contra me conspirare – I think some people in togas are plotting against me.

Magister Mundi sum! – I am the Master of the Universe!

At home

Mellita, domi adsum – Honey, I'm home.

Re vera, potas bene – Say, you really are drinking a lot.

Leaving

Fac ut vivas – Get a life.

Much have I learned from my teachers, more from my colleagues, but most from my students. The Talmud

Learning styles

While there is general agreement that there are different learning styles or multiple intelligences there is less agreement on what to call them and how to categorize them.

Howard Gardner lists seven intelligences and accelerated learning programmes that have generally followed this list:

○ Logical-mathematical intelligence: the ability to detect patterns, reason deductively, think logically and generally follow rules.

○ Linguistic intelligence: a mastery of language, these learners like words and express themselves through language, reading, writing and giving speeches.

○ Spatial intelligence: the ability to manipulate and create mental images in order to solve problems; learners are visual – they doodle, enjoy colour and relate to images and graphical elements; they learn through drawing diagrams, flow charts and maps.

○ Musical intelligence: the ability to recognize and compose musical pitches, tones, and rhythms; humming, singing and they enjoy multimedia projects.

○ Bodily-kinesthetic intelligence: the ability to use mental abilities to coordinate body movements; fidgeting, learning through role-play, movement and touching things.

○ Interpersonal: team players, they bounce ideas off others and help friends to solve problems through group discussions.

○ Intrapersonal intelligence: the ability to understand one's own feelings and motivations; may be loners, liking independent projects, journal writing and research.

Kathleen Butler offers five main categories and their learning needs:

○ Realistic: linear directions, specific assignments, charts, data and tools, orderly, practical and structured.

○ Analytical: intellectual dialogue, research topics, books, references, space to work alone, conceptual methods, reading and analysis.

- Pragmatic: real problems, hands on experience, team players and action methods.
- Personal: collaborative learning, working in harmony, time to work things through, personal interpretation, arts, music and writing.
- Divergent: excitement, fast-paced exploration, freedom of choice, original problem-solving and unconventional methods.

Wear your learning, like your watch, in a private pocket: and do not merely pull it out and strike it; merely to show that you have one.

Lord Chesterfield

Medical Emergencies | 9

 97 **First-aid – basic principles**

Aims

- ○ To rescue
- ○ To make safe
- ○ To resuscitate
- ○ To control breathing
- ○ To prevent worsening
- ○ Turn unconscious casualties to recovery position
- ○ Support fractures
- ○ Cool burns
- ○ Combat shock
- ○ Help recovery
- ○ Reassure
- ○ Don't underestimate the seriousness of the event
- ○ Obtain medical help
- ○ While waiting for medical help try to inform yourself of:
  - – *the history* – what happened, has it happened before?
  - – *the symptoms* – what the casualty is feeling or experiencing.
  - – *the signs* – what you, the first-aider, observes.
  - – *diagnosis* – this is best left to medical experts but you may help recovery if you can identify burns, epilepsy, fractures, diabetes.
  - – *treatment* – basic as above, and nothing which could injure the patient.
- ○ Don't move unless there is a very good reason.
- ○ Pass on relevant information and leave it to experienced medical personnel.

I might have dissected a frog five hundred times, but the 501st time I always see something I didn't before and it's the same thing with teaching students. You always see something new. Anne Frye

LIST 98 — Asthma

○ Keep calm.
○ Let the pupil sit in a comfortable position. Don't make him/her lie down.
○ Let the pupil use his/her usual inhaler (normally blue).
○ If no inhaler: call the parents, failing that call the family doctor.
○ Check attack is not severe.
○ Wait four to five minutes.
○ If symptoms disappear pupil can return to class.
○ If symptoms improve, but do not disappear, call parents and give another dose of inhaler.
○ Severe attack – any of the following symptoms and normal medication has no effect:
  – Pupil is so breathless he/she can't talk normally
  – Pulse is 120 per minute or more
  – Rapid breathing of 30 breaths per minute or more.
1 Call the family doctor
2 Ask the doctor to come immediately

Failing that:

3 Take the pupil to casualty. Warn the hospital that you're on your way.
4 Inform parents.
5 If the pupil has an emergency supply of oral steroids administer stated dose immediately.
6 Keep trying with usual reliever inhaler every five to ten minutes. Don't worry about overdosing.

Education is that which remains, if one has forgotten everything he learned in school.   Albert Einstein

Minor burns and scalds

Aim to

- ○ Stop the burning
- ○ Relieve pain
- ○ Minimize infection risk.
  1. Flood injured part with cold water for about ten minutes to stop burning and relieve pain.
  2. Gently remove jewellery, watches and constricting clothing from the affected area before any swelling begins.
  3. Cover affected area with a sterile dressing or any clean non-fluffy material. A polythene bag or cling film are suitable.

Do not

- ○ Use adhesive dressings
- ○ Break blisters
- ○ Apply cream or ointments
- ○ Cover burns to the face.

Our knowledge is the amassed thought and experience of innumerable minds: our language, our science, our religion, our opinions, our fancies we inherited.   Ralph Waldo Emerson

Epilepsy

Minor

Casualty appears to be daydreaming, staring blankly into the distance, may start to behave strangely – fiddling with clothing, saying strange things – possible loss of memory.

- Keep the person safe and away from other people.
- Talk calmly and quietly.
- Stay with the person until recovered and advise to see doctor.
- Watch for symptoms of a major fit which could follow.

Major

- Casualty loses consciousness and falls to the ground.
- Stiffens for a few seconds or twitches and jerks.
- Face becomes blue and congested.
- Breathing becomes difficult, possibly frothing at the mouth.
- Possible loss of bladder control.
- Muscles tighten or twitch, then relax.
- Person may remain unconscious for a few minutes.
- Patient regains consciousness, but is dazed and confused.
- Help the person from hurting themselves as they fall and place something soft under the head.
- Place patient in recovery position when jerking and twitching has stopped.

Do not

- Move patient unless there is danger.
- Try to hold them down.
- Put anything in the mouth.
- Try to wake the person.
- Give a drink until the patient is fully conscious.
- Send for an ambulance unless the casualty has another fit; has been injured by the fit; or takes longer than 15 minutes to recover full consciousness.

Only the educated are free.   Epictetus

Getting On – and Out

L I S T 101 Writing a job application

Keep your CV as a regularly updated computer file. This is your complete list of:

○ activities
○ responsibilities
○ qualifications and courses attended
○ dates and details.

From it you can extract that which is relevant to your precise application.

○ Write an honest list of your assets under the headings:
   – skills
   – knowledge and experience
   – achievements
   – examples to demonstrate your capacities. Where these are not evident in your CV make sure you emphasize your relevant assets if they are required by the job.
○ Note whether your application requires:
   – a letter or an application form
   – a CV.
○ Note what the job entails and what skills and experience are required.
○ If there is a personal profile describing the ideal candidate, try to match your experience, personality and skills to it.
○ If you don't match it completely, battle on; if you don't match it at all, try something else.
○ If there is a job profile try to match your experience and skills to it.

Good teaching is one-fourth preparation and three-fourths theatre.
Gail Godwin

Writing a CV

You are a teacher with skills that are wanted by, and transferable to, many non-education jobs. Think about what you have done and translate this into examples of skills which another employer will understand.

Demonstrate your initiative   Give examples of your motivation, enthusiasm and commitment. Show how you can move things along by your own energy.

Show how you have managed projects   If you have taken responsibility for a project, show how you laid out priorities, shared responsibilities among the team, managed time and met deadlines.

How you have solved problems   Show how you identified, coped, solved or worked round problems.

Can you organize and prioritize   Show how you plan ahead and meet targets.

Describe how you work in a team   Give examples of how you have worked successfully in a team, taking an appropriate role. If you can, show the different roles you have taken in different situations. You don't have to be a leader all the time; you need to know when to take a back seat too.

Convey your communication skills   Demonstrate how you successfully express yourself in a variety of ways. Are you able to persuade and convince?

Are you able and willing to continue learning   As a teacher you should understand learning for your students' sakes – but are you committed to continued learning for yourself? Are you flexible and willing to learn? Can you show you have undertaken in-service training?

How skilled are you in information technology?   Show what software you are familiar with and describe how you have used it successfully in your work.

The direction in which education starts a man will determine his future life.   Plato

Your other skills

- Do a skills audit.
- What do you like?
- What are you good at?
- Which skills are transferable?
- Remember that an 80 per cent match between your skills and those of a new job is good. Employers expect to give training.

Consider

- Communication
- IT
- People skills
- Management of people
- Management of change
- Literacy
- Subject specific skills for industry
- Learning and training skills
- Flexibility
- Motivation
- Independent working.

What aspects of your present job do you like and what don't you like? Express these in general and non-teaching terms, for example.

- Clear targets
- Clear boundaries
- Working with people
- Planned management
- Attitude to change
- Independence
- Working with young people
- Working in a team . . .

Education, like neurosis, begins at home.   Milton R. Sapirstein

Preparation for interviews

○ Think positive. Believe you can do it; be confident but not brash or loud; do not indulge in false modesty.

○ List twenty good things about yourself in relation to this job, refer to them at the interview and in your CV, and exemplify them in your interview behaviour.

○ Write a CV which emphasizes your good points and links to the job spec; include recent in-service training and be prepared to talk about its effectiveness. If you haven't had any, get on with it!

○ Prepare answers to the most likely questions, for example, 'Tell me about yourself and your recent experiences . . .'.

○ Compile a list of examples of your good practice – working effectively as part of a team, instigating change, dealing with a significant problem . . .

○ Dress comfortably but formally. Your clothes say a lot about you. Have an interview suit ready, comfortable shoes, a good haircut. If wearing a tie it could be a talking point, but not too showy; skirts should not be too short. Inspect candidates for jobs in your own workplace: what does their appearance say about them? Would you employ a man with a green or a brown suit?

○ If asked to teach a lesson ensure that you know the class age and ability, lesson length and timing, and equipment available. Choose a lesson that you are comfortable with, identify aims and outcomes, produce a lesson plan with National Curriculum links, which will differentiate learning. Suggest follow-up activities.

○ Turn up on time. Stay locally if there's a risk of lateness. Ask local people (landlady, publican, taxi driver) their impressions of the school. You might be warned off – or be able to drop a favourable comment at the interview.

Everyone who remembers his own educational experience remembers teachers, not methods and techniques. The teacher is the kingpin of the educational situation. The teacher makes and breaks programs.

Sidney Hook

L I S T 105   Common interview questions

○ Prepare responses to questions based on the job specification.

○ If you can't answer them ask if this really is the right job for you!

○ Have a 'critical friend' give you a mock interview.

  – Why do you want this job?

  – What qualities do you think you would bring with you to this job?

  – From what you have seen, what do you think could be improved in our school?

  – What do you most enjoy in your present job?

  – Why are you thinking of leaving?

  – How do you hope to benefit our school?

  – What are your strengths/weaknesses?

  – Describe a situation in which you have contributed to a team.

  – Give an example of a time when you successfully managed a difficult situation.

  – What was your biggest failure?

  – Where do you see yourself in five years?

  – Why should we employ you rather than any of the other candidates?

○ It is unlikely that you will be asked a dubious question – but be aware and wary of enquiries about:

  – Childcare

  – Partners

  – Sexual orientation

  – Race or ethnicity.

○ Don't forget that it is your choice whether you work there or not. You are perfectly within your rights to leave if you are unhappy with the situation.

Knowledge is of two kinds. We know a subject ourselves, or we know where we can find information upon it.   Samuel Johnson

Coping with tasks at interviews

Teaching a lesson

○ Prepare well for this artificial situation. Balance the desire to create an all-singing all-dancing show against the likelihood of equipment breakdown or unavailability. Balance the desire to show off your sparkling personality against the need to show learning activities in the pupils.

○ Heads of departments and deputies might have an in-tray exercise or show how they would cope with a variety of situations:

– *paperwork* – how do you prioritize, deal with deadlines, delegate, prepare for the introduction of changes . . .?

– *parents* – enquiring about an incident in the classroom of a teacher in your department, checking on homework policy, worrying about setting for their child, believing their child's side of the story against that of a teacher, bullying incidents . . .

– *colleagues* – how you supervise them, how you encourage them, how you work with them, give them responsibility, delegate to them, provide in-service training for them . . .

– *students* – discipline, behaviour, attendance, performance, differentiation, reporting . . .

– *events* – more likely for heads and deputies, for example, how you would react to the death of a pupil, a fire in a school building, a breakdown in trust within the governing body, drug trafficking within school . . .

Education is not a problem. Education is an opportunity.

Lyndon B. Johnson

L I S T 107   Coping with questions at interviews

○ Always answer honestly, although it may be wise to be succinct.
  - Don't make promises you can't keep.
  - Avoiding mention of negative relationships in your previous job.
  - Don't go on about too many personal experiences.
  - Saying too much is more likely to raise doubts about you than saying too little.
○ Listen to the question.
○ Reflect briefly on the question.
○ Clarify the question if necessary.
○ Respond succinctly to the question.
○ Wait for the next one.
○ Remember your interview starts from the moment you enter the building and you are on show throughout the day.
○ Look interested and alert.
○ Sit straight not slumped.
○ Engage eye contact with all the interviewers, especially, though not solely, the immediate questioner.
○ Clasp hands loosely in your lap. Don't fiddle!
○ Avoid hinting that this job is just a stepping stone to the next and better one.
○ Be prepared to ask a question at the end of your interview.
  'Do you have any questions?'
  - 'No thank you, I've been given an excellent tour and I'd like to thank you for an interesting day'; or
  - 'Yes, I wonder if you could tell me the school's policy on supporting long-term training opportunities'.
○ Don't ask a selfish question which suggests that you're in the job only for money or status. Suggest how *you* can help *them* not how you can get something for yourself.

Give a child an inch and he'll think he's a ruler.　　　Sam Levenson

Sucking up to your superiors

- Offer to take an extra-curricular club or team.
- Offer to take part in working parties/management groups on a voluntary/observer basis.
- Stay late and bump into the Head as you leave (this involves finding out from the secretary when he/she is likely to leave).
- Start doing a job voluntarily in the hope you'll be noticed and get paid for it.
- Make yourself invaluable.
- Don't become a union rep until you've established yourself.
- Make an INSET plan which includes curriculum updating, new initiatives and management training.
- Find out the head's weaknesses (ICT? Working with the PTA or the Chair of Governors? Analysing statistics?) and help him/her out.
- Prepare one-off presentation lessons to impress visitors.
- Make your classroom a shrine to education, a living learning lounge (or at least put it about that it is).

. . . our knowledge can only be finite, while our ignorance must necessarily be infinite.   Karl Popper

LIST 109 Continuing professional development

Personal experience can be extended by:

- Team teaching with other colleagues.
- Taking opportunities to teach a wider range of age groups, topics and syllabuses.
- Sitting in on curriculum meetings (by invitation).
- Volunteering for working parties.
- Attending courses run by the LEA or commercial organizations.
- Visiting other schools.
- Shadowing other teachers.

Educational research and news can be found via either your local education institute, teachers' centre or on the web at the following locations:

- http://www.gtce.org.uk/research
  Information about research at the General Teaching Council, more general research information and a Research of the Month feature.
- http://eppi.ioe.ac.uk
  The Evidence for Policy and Practice Information and Co-ordinating Centre (EPPI-Centre) leads to The Research Evidence in Education Library (REEL). A centralized resource for people wishing to undertake systematic reviews of research in education and those wishing to use reviews to inform policy and practice.
- http://195.194.2.34/research/research.asp
  The National Foundation for Educational Research (NFER) maintains a comprehensive research portfolio comprising over 100 projects at any given time.
- www.professionaldevelopmentreview.org.uk/links.html
  The National Union of Teachers Continuing Professional Development Group.
- www.bera.ac.uk
  British Educational Research Association.
- www.ncsl.org.uk/
  National College for School Leadership.
- www.tlrp.org
  Teaching and Learning Research Council, University of Cambridge, Faculty of Education.

○ ioewebserver.ioe.ac.uk/ioe/index.html
  University of London, Institute of Education.

Also read *The Times Educational Supplement* regularly (and not just the Jobs sections . . .) at www.tes.co.uk/.

There is nothing on earth intended for innocent people so horrible as a school. It is in some respects more cruel than a prison.   George Bernard Shaw

Thinking of leaving teaching?

Teaching can be a great, satisfying, stimulating career, but it can also be depressing, fatiguing, dispiriting and mentally draining.

Is the problem:

- Your specific job?
- Your job in general?
- Other aspects in your life?

(Your job might be the cause of your misery – but it could be the salvation of your life when other things fall apart.)

○ Visit a careers guidance counsellor. Try www.iacmp.org.uk.
○ Ask yourself big questions such as:
  - What would you do if you found you only had one year to live?
  - What would you do if you were made redundant?
  - What's your big dream? If you won the lottery tomorrow where would you go, what would you do?
  - If you looked back on your life on your death bed what would you regret not doing?
  - What would you do if you knew you couldn't fail – or if money was no object?
○ Ask a friend or colleague to quiz you about your aspirations, jobs, dreams, hopes and desires. Ask them to tell you honestly what you are talking about when your eyes light up and you start to get really animated. What is it that really turns you on?
○ Build a set of contacts – people you like, who you'd like to work for, who could set you off in the right direction, who might be useful.
○ Find someone who is supportive and honest and who believes in you. Keep talking to them to get the confidence to get on with your new life.
○ Keep your CV up to date and review it regularly.

To learn is to change. Education is a process that changes the learner.
George B. Leonard

Signs you have become bitter and twisted and it's time to go

○ When you hate all kids, not just a deserving few.

○ When you start saying 'We did that in 1976 – and it didn't work then!'

○ When more and more of your staffroom conversations start, 'Do you remember old what's his name?'.

○ When you comment, 'Of course the previous head was far better . . .'.

○ When you call new rooms by their old, pre-rebuilding, names.

○ When you call Year 10 'The fourth year'.

○ When colleagues leave your customary space in the car park empty for you.

○ When your heart sinks instead of lifts as you walk into the first lesson with a new class.

○ When you talk to pupils about their elder brothers and sisters.

○ When you taught their parents.

○ When promoted colleagues pop in on a visit and ask, 'Are you still here?'.

○ When at a rare party people ask what you do – and you're embarrassed to say.

○ When people ask what you do, you say you're a teacher and they look embarrassed and change the subject.

○ When new kids say 'Who's that grumpy old man?'.

○ When you arrive late and leave early.

○ When you look at your stack of old mark books and you realize you can tell exactly where you were – and with which pupils – at any time – and on any day of the school year – for the last 25 years.

I touch the future. I teach.   Christa McAuliffe

Alternative careers

Teaching is not the only thing you can do – far from it! But teaching for a few years can lead to you becoming institutionalized. Holidays are appealing especially if you have a young family. Nevertheless it is good for everyone to reassess their skills. Some may consider how another career could use those skills in other ways.

In addition to your subject-specific knowledge you are likely to have many of the following:

○ the ability to communicate effectively in a variety of ways – writing, speaking, describing; individually, in small and large groups
○ literacy and numeracy
○ practical IT skills
○ the ability to plan and to carry out your plan and work as a team
○ the ability to relate sensitively to people
○ independence and self-motivation
○ flexibility.

All of these are required skills for many jobs outside of the classroom. Skilled communicators are required everywhere.

Consider setting up your own business or working for someone else:

○ training
○ consultancy
○ inspection
○ production of resources and materials
○ publishing
○ part-time individual tutoring or adult education
○ examination invigilation (not just schools)
○ Examination Boards
○ counselling.

Our progress as a nation can be no swifter than our progress in education.
John Fitzgerald Kennedy

Leaving gracefully

○ Leave a good impression when you leave, not a sour taste.

○ Don't let a few last weeks of resentment or idleness spoil several years of hard work.

○ Who needs to know first that you're going? Manage the news sensitively.

○ Never publicly admit that you can't stand your boss or your colleagues:
  - Say how much you learned from them.
  - Tell them you're sorry to go; thank them for everything.
  - Hope that they'll give you a good reference in the future.

○ Document as much as you can:
  - Place projects in the hands of those you trust or those who will take over.
  - Leave things tidy – metaphorically and literally.

○ Don't promise to be on call if they ever need you.

○ Make sure that the people you like and trust know where you're going and how they can contact you.

○ If you're going freelance, make explicit contacts.

○ At your leaving do, stay sober and keep your leaving speech short.

○ Keep working to the end. The pupils still need teaching as best you can.

○ Don't give up or have regrets towards the end, just think positively about your future.

We just must not, we just cannot afford the great waste that comes from the neglect of a single child.
Lyndon B. Johnson

Leaving speeches

Length of speech

- Leaving speeches should not be long. This depends on how many others are leaving and how long you've been at the school.
- Five minutes should be enough for all but the most senior colleague.
- Real old-timers deserve an additional formal meal at another time.

Speeches should:

- Be positive yet quite brief.
- Be witty, if you are good at that sort of thing, straight if you're not.
- Give thanks for the opportunity to work with colleagues, rather than boast about one's own achievements. Leave the latter modestly to the person seeing you off.
- Recall and praise colleagues past and present.
- Recall pupils of previous years in a mainly positive way; the mere mention of an infamous character can be an effective crowd pleaser.
- Appeal to the common experience of teachers in that school.

Speeches should avoid

- Recrimination and criticizing anyone (pupil or colleague) by name.
- Cynicism.
- Getting your own back (it doesn't work, and people will think less of you ever after).
- Length and tedium.
- Too many 'in' jokes, which will be meaningless to newcomers.
- Self-written poetry, especially if:
  - (a) you think it's very funny
  - (b) you are not naturally gifted
  - (c) if your idea of poetry is short lines of rhyming couplets.

One looks back with appreciation to the brilliant teachers, but with gratitude to those who touched our human feelings. The curriculum is so much necessary raw material, but warmth is the vital element for the growing plant and for the soul of the child. Carl Jung

Leaving gifts

Attendance

Even if you may be embarrassed by or emotional about leave-takings you must be there; it gives others their right to see you off, an important rite of passage for all of you.

Gifts from the leaver

- ○ A set of matching mugs for the staffroom or department base will be well received.
- ○ Anything else of practical use to staff, but not too ostentatious, will be appreciated. For example:
  - – cakes and sticky buns for all
  - – contribution to a round of drinks, or a large jug
  - – a clock for the staffroom is unlikely to be welcomed from anyone except a departing head
  - – an inexpensive electric urn, if the staffroom fights over kettles and coffee
  - – a large sign concreted into the car park proclaiming RESERVED FOR THE HEAD OF ENGLISH (or whichever post you are leaving)
  - – lifers might consider setting aside something in their will
  - – a comfortable chair for the staffroom
  - – a bench for a secluded but sunny area away from children
  - – contributions for books for the school library will be better received than the remains of your own library
  - – a sum to provide a prize for your favourite aspect of the curriculum.
- ○ Gifts for the leaving teacher should be in proportion to the length of service and should match their interests.
- ○ Prints and photographs accompanied by book or gardening tokens are usually safe.
- ○ Particular preferences should be enquired about well in advance.

Children are unpredictable. You never know what inconsistency they're going to catch you in next. Franklin P. Jones

Reasons why you work (no really, there are some)

Considering a change in career; you might go back to basics and ask just why you work and whether any alternative career could fulfil you.

- ○ Stimulation
- ○ Sense of purpose
- ○ Making a difference
- ○ A challenge
- ○ Prestige
- ○ Companionship
- ○ Inner peace
- ○ Money
- ○ Excitement
- ○ Responsibility
- ○ To travel
- ○ Sense of self-worth
- ○ To contribute
- ○ Learning new skills
- ○ Social acceptance
- ○ Psychological and personal development
- ○ Working as a team to a common goal
- ○ To experience variety

Add any others you can think of and place these in order of importance to you. Are you experiencing these in your present job? If not, what can you do instead which lets you experience these priorities?

Teach the young people how to think, not what to think.   Sidney Sugarman

Good INSET opportunities

INSET isn't just a set of courses, it's professional training through experience – your own and others. Treat every education experience as an INSET opportunity.

○ Good course providers are only as good as the people giving the training – but look out for SFE, Key Stage and Lighthouse.

○ Shadow one pupil for the day. You'll learn more about the way a school works from that day than you would in any education lecture.

○ Shadow a teacher for a day. Newly qualified teachers (NQTs) will learn tricks, strategies and techniques that are rarely written down formally.

○ Once in a while do your break duty proactively, talk to pupils about their day instead of hiding behind a cup of coffee.

○ Sit in on pastoral interviews between parents, children and pastoral staff.

○ Arrange a week's exchange/work experience at another school and prepare a report for both schools on comparisons and contrasts.

○ Attend Examination Board meetings on reviews and feedback on exam papers.

○ At any course or meeting make an effort to share experiences and opinions with other teachers.

○ Email educational discussion groups.

○ Offer to be a mentor to groups of children – the more able, less able, the victims, the low achieving children; whichever you feel comfortable with.

○ Offer to mentor an ITT student. This will force you to reflect on your own practice. This is a good, but sometimes scary, thing to do!

It is, in fact, nothing short of a miracle that the modern methods of instruction have not yet entirely strangled the holy curiosity of inquiry.

Albert Einstein